Tending the Wild Garden

Find digital resources at
www.wjkbooks.com/TendingTheWildGarden
that provide inspiration for preachers, images
for use in worship and study, and more.

Tending the Wild Garden

*Growing in the Fruit
of the Spirit*

Eugenia Anne Gamble

WESTMINSTER
JOHN KNOX PRESS
LOUISVILLE • KENTUCKY

First edition
Published by Westminster John Knox Press
Louisville, Kentucky

24 25 26 27 28 29 30 31 32 33—10 9 8 7 6 5 4 3 2 1

Unless otherwise indicated, Scripture quotations are from the New Revised Standard Version Updated Edition, copyright © 2021 National Council of Churches of Christ in the United States of America. Used by permission. All rights reserved worldwide. Scripture quotations marked CEB are from the Common English Bible, © 2011 Common English Bible, and are used by permission.

Book design by Drew Stevens
Cover design by Luísa Dias

Library of Congress Cataloging-in-Publication Data

Names: Gamble, Eugenia, 1953-, author.
Title: Tending the wild garden : growing in the fruit of the
    spirit / Eugenia Anne Gamble.
Description: First edition. | Louisville, Kentucky : Westminster John Knox
    Press, [2024] | Includes bibliographical references. | Summary:
    "Explores the true meaning of each attribute in Paul's "fruit of the
    spirit" list, helping readers overcome any shame, guilt, or
    misunderstandings and showing how we can effectively manage the weeds
    that threaten the fruit's flourishing"-- Provided by publisher.
Identifiers: LCCN 2024016407 (print) | LCCN 2024016408 (ebook) | ISBN
    9780664268602 (paperback) | ISBN 9781646983865 (ebook)
Subjects: LCSH: Fruit of the Spirit. | Gifts, Spiritual--Biblical teaching.
    | Christian life--Biblical teaching. | Spiritual healing--Biblical
    teaching. | Bible. Epistles of Paul--Criticism, interpretation, etc.
Classification: LCC BV4501.3 .G362 2024 (print) | LCC BV4501.3 (ebook) |
    DDC 248.4--dc23/eng/20240520
LC record available at https://lccn.loc.gov/2024016407
LC ebook record available at https://lccn.loc.gov/2024016408

Most Westminster John Knox Press books are available at special quantity discounts when purchased in bulk by corporations, organizations, and special-interest groups. For more information, please e-mail SpecialSales@wjkbooks.com.

To my amazing colleagues and first readers
Kim Vanbrimmer and Char Mace and
the unbeatable team at Westminster John Knox Press

But the fruit of the Spirit is love, joy, peace, patience, kindness, goodness, faithfulness, gentleness, and self-control. There is no law against things like this.
Galatians 5:22–23 (CEB)

CONTENTS

INTRODUCTION

Before every person there marches an angel
proclaiming, "Behold, the image of God!"
— Jewish Proverb

A s children, we are sometimes asked what we are going to be when we grow up. We usually answer with what we are going to do: a role we want to play, like doctor, firefighter, teacher, writer, chemist, mom, or dad. As adults, when we meet new people, someone invariably asks us what we do, and we rattle off a job title or make jokes about retirement. What if, instead, we spent a bit more of our time thinking about the being inside of our doing? It is easy in the crush of responsibility and activity to lose sight of the part of us that is deepest and most true, the part that is in constant communion with the Spirit. This book is designed to help you become more aware of the "being" part of you in relationship with the Holy Spirit that lives within you.

Lingering a while on the apostle Paul's provocative image of the fruit of the Spirit (Gal. 5:22–23a), we can discover anew what it means to *be* a Spirit-indwelt, deeply loved child in whom God makes God's home.

1

Everything I write about in this book is already inside you. It is not something that you have to search for high and low. The Spirit and its fruit are already working away, feeding and flourishing, whether you are aware of that work or not. The fruit is within you, whether you cooperate with it or not. The fruit of the Spirit is what God *does* in us, because that is who God *is* in us.

Notice that the fruit of the Spirit is referred to in the singular. It is "fruit" and not "fruits." All the aspects that Paul mentions are part of one whole. When we explore the fruit of the Spirit, we pay attention to that which is most deeply planted within our souls. It is not, at heart, an action plan for us to master. It is not even a set of beliefs to which we acquiesce. It is a loving awakening to the ways that Spirit works in us and what that healing and ripening work produces.

To engage with the fruit of the Spirit is not just to understand or to better recognize that fruit, as useful as that may be. It is, rather, to deepen our relationship with our source, the wild untamed Spirit of God, who brings to maturity a way of life that is both countercultural and immediately recognizable as home. To awaken to Spirit fruit is not to become other than we are in order to fix ourselves, our lives, or our problems. It is to truly *be* ourselves. It is to be the grace-blessed, Spirit-inhabited, divinely loved and strengthened beings that we were created to be.

When we recognize ourselves as dwelling places of the divine Spirit, we realize that we do not acquire the fruit of the Spirit like a trophy at a soccer match. Our task is to tend the Spirit's garden, ripen in the Spirit's ways, taste the fruit, get to know its richness, and create an environment for the Spirit to express herself in us and through us. The more aware we become of the Spirit's presence and fruit, the better we are able to live out of their beauty.

THINGS TO REMEMBER
AS YOU STUDY

A couple of things may be helpful for you as you enter into these reflections. First of all, I invite you to use a different lens from the one through which you may most often look at instructions in the Bible. We often see the Bible as urging moral characteristics and choices that we must embrace and allow to guide our behavior. There are many cases in which that is perfectly true. For this exploration, however, I invite you to set aside the heavy need to master the fruit in your behavior. Set aside as well all the attendant judgment, shame, and desire for control. Try on a new set of glasses that contain the dual lenses of *awakening* and *surrendering*. Try to entertain the notion that the fruit is not a set of morals to be checked off in order to feel safe from God's wrath or displeasure. Nor is it a checklist to manage in order to be a faithful disciple. Rather, acknowledge, for a moment, that the Spirit is already bringing to fruit every possible good thing in, and through, you. You are asked simply to clear the ground, expand your vision, release, and share what the Spirit produces in and through you.

To explore the fruit of the Spirit in this way, it will be helpful to reframe your image of God from police officer to midwife. If the Spirit's job is to keep you in line, that is one thing. If the Spirit's job is to bring new life to delivery within you, that is another thing altogether. Both roles can certainly be useful at times. For now, consider that God is not an offended monarch on a faraway throne who is perpetually disgusted with us hapless mortals. Rather, consider that God calls us to the joy of God's presence by inviting us to discover our deepest desires, our most authentic selves, and God's own immense power and beauty. Let God do the work of bringing forth fruit in you with carrots and not sticks.

A second thing that will be helpful in this study is to develop comfort with paradoxes. They are at the heart of the spiritual life. The Bible is full of them, most notably that the route to true and everlasting life is through physical death and the many little deaths along the way. In approaching the fruit of the Spirit, we discover that trying to master them never works. In my opinion, no one ever embodies the fruit of the Spirit by trying harder. At the same time, we have some responsibility for the inner work of garden tending. We cannot work our way to surrender, yet we must work hard to create an environment for surrender. Both of those things are true at the same time even though they may not seem to be.

It will be helpful as you read not to worry about or rate your progress. Those are not categories of thought in the Spirit's garden. Growth and ripening are the categories here, and they often happen in fits and starts. Fret not! You are not a failure. You are on a journey, and a lifelong one at that. The fruit, in each of its aspects, is not intended to be an intermittent outpouring but a settled state of our being. As with any ripening, that takes time. Jesus says, "Abide in me as I abide in you." Still, as with all blooming things, there are seasons of abundance and seasons of waiting for new growth. Our job when we are overflowing, and when we seem fallow, is to tend and to wait.

A third thing that may take some getting used to is the limitation of the English language for talking about the Spirit. What pronouns are appropriate for talk of the Spirit? In the Hebrew Scriptures, also called the Old Testament, the Spirit (Hebrew *ruach*) is feminine. In the New Testament, the pronouns applied to the Spirit (Greek *pneuma*) are neuter. While the Scriptures in English most often use masculine pronouns for the Godhead, and masculine pronouns are always appropriate when speaking of Jesus' life on earth, the pronouns lose their meaning when

Jesus ascends in fullness to the Godhead. In that broad, undefinable, unitive state, gendered language can only limit and confuse. All metaphors for the divine break down when pushed too far. God is not gendered but is reflected back to us in all human beings, made in the image of God (Gen. 1:27).

Still, to use the pronouns "she" and "it" for the Spirit, as the Bible does, in our day can light people's hair on fire and send them into the streets screaming heresy. Or, more often, they cause a reader to grind her teeth, mutter something about being politically correct, as if that were a bad thing, and check out of the book altogether. Due to these challenges of language, I avoid pronouns for the Spirit as much as possible. When that becomes so awkward that the point I'm trying to make gets lost in the construction, I use "It" or "She" in accordance with the Scripture. Let these pronouns roll around in your heart and soul. Taste them. They are not heretical. They are not political. They are biblical, and you may find that they have healing work to do in you as well.

THE CONTEXT

I have always had a come-here, go-away, come-here, go-away relationship with the apostle Paul, the author of the letter we consider in this book. His lavish insistence on the power of grace and the capacity for personal and communal transformation draw me like a hummingbird to nectar. His culture-bound misogyny and his blinders to his own blinders (like our own) make me want to run screaming for the soft comfort of more symbolic and mystical texts. Still, even in my go-away moments, I find that if I stay and cut slits in my own blinders, I can see a mystical explosion of divine presence at work in his words. In the few verses that this book explores, I find just such an explosion.

Most of Paul's letters are correspondence with people he knows and churches he has founded. Such was the case with Galatians. In 25 BCE, the Romans created an imperial province called Galatia. It included the original kingdom of Galatia and extended southward to include portions of six other regions, including the cities of Antioch, Iconium, Lystra, and Derbe. Much of the region was in what we now know as Turkey and parts of Greece. Perhaps this letter is addressed to one particular congregation in that area. More likely, it is addressed to a group of churches that are all struggling with similar issues.

What issue led to this letter? We don't exactly know, but it is clear that Paul was furious with them! First of all, some were claiming that Paul could not have been an apostle because he did not meet the criteria set out by Peter when Jesus' followers decided to replace Judas (Acts 1:15–26). Paul spends the early part of his letter defending and defining his apostleship.

What was of most concern to him, however, was theological and not personal. Apparently, some of the Jewish Christians believed that Christ was sent for the Jewish people only. They had been raised to despise Gentiles, so much so that they believed the call to care for the neighbor referred only to their Jewish neighbors. In some quarters the hatred was so intense that Gentiles were thought to have been created just to fuel the fires of hell. These more strident views were difficult to tame completely even in Paul's early mission. While Paul welcomed Gentiles, some in the Galatian church feared that if Gentiles were allowed to be Christians it would somehow negate God's covenant with the people of Israel. That was a bridge too far.

And yet, Gentiles were coming to faith in Christ. What were they to do? Their answer was to insist that the Gentile converts first become Jews and that the males be circumcised. They thought they were being both generous and righteous. Paul, on the other hand, saw this as a first step back into the full requirements of the law.

The issue for him was justification (how people are saved). The Jewish Christians said that Christ (grace) and circumcision (law-keeping) gave one right standing before God. Paul maintained that Christ alone does that. The bulk of the letter makes the argument that we are free in Christ from the requirements of the law. In the verses that will guide our reflection, Galatians 5:16–23, Paul gives his beautiful description of Spirit-filled life. He paints a picture of life without Christ as center and what the fruit of the Spirit brings about in a Christ-centered believer and in the beloved community. He is very much concerned about the judgmental and fractious spirit that has grown up in the church. People are taking sides and talking badly about each other. He will have no more of it! The Christian life is to be marked by certain qualities, and nothing more or less than that will do.

ABOUT THE SPIRIT'S GARDEN

When I was a little girl, I often had a hard time breathing. I remember it being especially difficult in the spring when the thick pine pollen coated the front porch of our home, the cars in the drive, and the lungs in the house. Sometimes, when the air was thick and the infections in my lungs persistent, as I lay in bed struggling to breathe, my mother would lie across the foot of my bed and tell me stories of Seagrove Beach, Florida.

Seagrove was, in those days, a tiny, barely developed spot on the Gulf coast where the waters were emerald green and warm, and the sands sugar white. It always seemed that I breathed a little easier there. Maybe the ocean breezes swept the pollen far inland and away. I'm not sure. What I do remember is that when I was desperately sick, Mama lay at the foot of my bed and reminded me of Seagrove. She described it in elaborate detail, the water, the sand, the shells, the beach bonfires with hot dogs on a palmetto frond that Daddy sharpened to a fine point. She promised that if I would hold on, we would go there. I remember closing my eyes and breathing deeply, as deeply as I could, and imaging myself running along the shore in the sunshine with my eyes closed and arms outstretched. It was my vision of wholeness.

The fruit of the Spirit is Paul's vision of wholeness. In Christ, we live in and share a garden, an orchard, a vineyard of beauty, bounty, and love that produces fruit to feed and change the world. Paul's language of the fruit of the Spirit describes the outward manifestations of an interior life lived in communion with the Spirit. Like the mysterious transformation of a seed into a fruitful plant, the product of this Spirit-filled life will be obvious to all and feed both our souls and the Spirit-starved world around us.

For many of us, the Spirit's garden is elusive, far more elusive than a beach trip for a sick child—and just as alluring. We may sense that there is something more that we are meant to live. We may realize that the choices and habits we have developed do not tend our souls effectively, but we don't quite know how to proceed. We have been given the passcode (grace through faith), but we seem flummoxed by the operating system. Too often we just give up and go back to what we understand and think we can control, while the garden runs wild and untended within us.

The Spirit within us blossoms in the ways Paul lists even when we are unaware, but it blossoms extravagantly when attended to and given what is needed to flourish. Tending is not the same thing as thinking about or learning about the fruit. To tend, we have to enter the garden. We have to deal with the pests, smell the fragrance of the blooms, and, above all else, refuse to give up. It is a process. The fruit of the Spirit is a sign of union and not a template for mastery. People who do not really believe that transformation is possible will rarely experience the fruit of the Spirit as regular aspects of their lives. They may learn to mimic the actions, but that is like trying to eat the plastic fruit on your grandmother's dining table.

In Paul's letters, he offers us a number of different lists of *gifts* of the Spirit. Those lists include such things as prophecy, exhortation, tongues, wisdom, knowledge, and the like. Spiritual gifts are particular ways the Spirit chooses to work with us and within us. We do not choose them. They are bestowed on particular people for particular purposes. The *fruit* of the Spirit is a different concept altogether. Fruit is the product or the result of something—the evidence. In Matthew 7:15–20, in a short teaching about discernment, Jesus tells us that we will know the truth of people by the fruit of their lives.

The fruit of the Spirit is the image of God most apparent in us. John Duns Scotus, a thirteenth-century Scottish mystic, talked about the "univocity of being," the idea that words used to describe God mean the same thing when used to describe humans. Therefore, the different aspects of the fruit are qualities of God, planted deeply within us to allow us to be who God most uniquely and specifically created us to be and to demonstrate that way of being to the world, thereby calling each person into their divine fullness. The fruit of the Spirit is the *imago Dei*—the image of God—for us to discover, recover, and live out.

I think of the fruit of the Spirit as streams of the Spirit's energy and values for the nourishing of the soul and of the world. We are the delivery system and the beneficiaries of the fruit's transforming power. Tending the wild garden is not about being a better person or a better Christian. It is about being a better expression of the One who dwells within us and even prays within us for our own needs and the needs of a "fruit"-hungry world. The fruit of the Spirit is grace in skin.

TENDING HOLY GROUND

Paul's image of the fruit of the Spirit gives us a lens through which we experience the radiant heart of God that is always loving, always relational, always moral, and always mysterious. Because that is the terrain we will till in this book, be aware as you study that you will be on holy ground. You might want to light a candle as you read, reminding yourself that your study is actually a form of prayer. You might want to take off your shoes, remembering that the bush is always burning. You might want to actually eat a piece of fruit, reminding yourself of the wondrous way the Spirit restores our Eden. Take your time. Gardens always take time.

In my own Reformed tradition, there has historically been a preference for the practical, social, and communal aspects of piety, over the more mystical and strictly personal experiences of spiritual life. Both of those aspects are important to me and have provided grace upon grace for me all my life. For that reason, this book will offer suggestions for both a grounded practical piety using what we learn of the fruit of the Spirit and glimpses of a personal and experiential practice as well.

Each chapter includes a look at obstacles to the maturing of the fruit in our lives. As all of us who have read the story of the first garden in Genesis 3 know, there is a snake in the garden, and one has to deal with it. Obstacles need to be addressed. Weeds need to be pulled. Each chapter ends with six days' worth of Scriptures and questions for individual reflection or group discussion. My prayer is that, as you tend the wild garden within you, you will bear the Spirit's perfectly ripened fruit for your life, your family, and our hungry world.

CHAPTER 1

THE SPIRIT
OF THE GARDEN

We little know how much wildness is in us.
—John Muir

How do we talk about the fruit of the Spirit without turning the text into a cosmic to-do list destined to leave us feeling shamed, discouraged, or self-righteous about our own spiritual maturity? Perhaps it is best to start by considering the Spirit who raises a garden within us and invites us to welcome and tend it.

Speaking of the Holy Spirit is notoriously difficult. It is often like trying to nail smoke or describe something you thought you glimpsed, but when you turned around, it was gone. Questions about the Trinity and how the persons of the Godhead relate to one another and behave are guaranteed to make seminary interns cry and seasoned pastors squirm. Do we try to talk about the persons as personas, masks that the one Great One wears? Do we try to explain with examples like water, ice, and steam? Do we talk in terms of relationship, with ourselves as the ultimate referent, *our* Father, *our* brother, *our* indweller? Do we try to satisfy our inquiring minds by sorting the persons of the Trinity into discrete roles—creator, redeemer, sustainer? This inquiry can be captivating and not without usefulness. It does, of necessity, eventually break down. They are One even as there are, we believe, spaces between them, places where they both interact and interpenetrate. Even the ancient believers who loved nothing more, after Constantine's command, than to nail down the dictates of the faith could muster nothing more than "I believe in the Holy Spirit" for the Apostles' Creed.

So rather than plumb theological waters too deep for me, I want to spend time in this chapter considering the *experience* of the Spirit, both in Scripture and in our personal lives, so that we may ponder what those experiences can teach us as we practice tending the garden of the Spirit's fruit within us.

GOD'S SPIRIT IN THE OLD TESTAMENT

In the Hebrew Scriptures, where there is, obviously, no articulated doctrine of the Trinity, God's Spirit is still found everywhere. The word we usually translate as "spirit" in Hebrew is *ruach*. It is also the word for air, wind, breath, breeze, courage, and even temper. To be overwhelmed is to be breathless or spirit-less. This word is also used to describe the invisible, intangible, and fleeting quality of life itself in a person. Spirit is what distinguishes a living thing from a nonliving thing. In the Hebrew Scriptures, life begins when breath begins. So Spirit is always present, vivifying, elusive, unseen, but nonetheless felt.

A concrete example in the Hebrew Scriptures of what Christians call the Holy Spirit comes in the opening verses of the book of Genesis (1:2). There we see the *ruach* of

God moving over the waters of chaos, the formlessness and emptiness, and contemplating how to pull back those waters so that creation can emerge and take form. *Ruach* is the force of divine energy moving to create in love and for love. In these first verses of the Bible, we find the Spirit in pregnant wonder, imagining new life, bringing it to birth, releasing everything to love.

The Spirit is the divine energy of God that plants the garden of life for us and in us. It is God's divine power to the fullest. *Ruach* sorts light from darkness, brings things into being at the right time, spins planets, and sets boundaries around the chaos. This is not a picture of a meek, sweet Spirit that makes us feel better. *Ruach* is fierce. Rabbi Abraham Heschel once said, "God is not nice. God is not an uncle. God is an earthquake."[1] When we consider such aspects of the Spirit's fruit as gentleness and self-control, we remember, too, that there is a bit of fierceness there. *Ruach* is an earthquake.

So, *ruach* is the fierce creative spirit that brings life to life. She is also the one who never gives up. *Ruach* is not discouraged by the chaos and emptiness of any age and is always bringing new life even when the ground seems fallow and there are no ingredients left with which to work. *Ruach* needs no ingredients. She is the ingredient. *Ruach* is undaunted by division and even destruction. Recently, amid the horrors of war in Ukraine, I saw pictures of high school students in their prom dresses posing amid the rubble of their destroyed school. Even in the rubble of human brokenness, *ruach* weaves defiant joy.

We see the wild, indomitable Spirit again in Ezekiel 37, where the fierce power of the Spirit and the Spirit's commitment to individuals and to communities is on full display. Throughout much of the book of Ezekiel, the prophet declares the doom of the coming exile of the people. He tells of Jerusalem's fall and the temple's destruction. For him, the entire community, and God's promise with it, is like a vast valley of dried bones. Israel's inability to live as God intended has left it vulnerable and decimated. There is nothing left but death. Not even hope is left in the dried bones. Yet even at the moment when the worst happens, both internally and externally, the prophet tells us that the Spirit never gives up. The Spirit needs nothing from us, no potential, no goodness, not even hope. All the Spirit needs is her own fierce love that leads to life. When human beings give up in the presence of devastation and the consequences of faithlessness, the Spirit does not. God brings life from death. Verse 14 says, "I will put my spirit within you, and you shall live, and I will place you on your own soil." The Spirit's very breath is the life force of all creation. The Spirit shakes the ground on which we stand, and that which we thought was solid, or dead and done, is once again malleable.

A second understanding of Spirit from Hebrew faith is Shekinah. While this word does not appear in the Old Testament, rabbis in the Talmudic period used this term to refer to God's intimate presence and special bond with God's people and God's world. Often talked about as a kind of ethereal light, the Shekinah surrounds people with holiness, mystery, and intimacy. The understanding of Shekinah is built on experiences such as the assurance in Exodus 29:45–46 that God will dwell with the people in a steadfast and experiential way. The Shekinah is God's mysterious yet intimate embrace.

My earliest memory is one I have come to associate with the Shekinah. Some of this "memory" comes to me from family lore, but some of it is as distinct as if happening right this moment. The context was the funeral of my paternal grandmother, when I was only three years old. My grandfather had died the year before I was born. My parents then left their own little home and moved into the family home where my father had been born. My grandmother was a brittle diabetic who never fully recovered from the death of her husband. She loved me wildly, and I her. Each morning as breakfast was served to her in bed, I was wheeled in a stroller to her bedside, where she fed me bacon tidbits and crusts of toast with a little egg dripping from the edges.

In those days in the Deep South, funerals were often held in the home, so my grandmother's casket was set before the fireplace in the living room. Somewhere in all the planning, the decision was made that I was too young to attend, so I was taken across the street to my cousin's house. That is where my memory becomes distinct. I don't remember which older cousin had me by the hand, just that my arm was lifted high in that clutch. When we had safely crossed the street, I stopped and turned back to look at my house. I remember seeing the mourners in their black suits, the women in simple hats with small eye veils and black gloves, walking up the walkway and being welcomed into the home. Suddenly, I saw a bright golden light surrounding the house. It was spiky and almost pulsating. It looked a bit like the crown on the Statue of Liberty, dancing. I stared at it in wonderment. I was not afraid. It seemed like the most natural thing in the world. I knew that it was God, without a doubt. And I knew that God was surrounding and holding my family and my grandmother. Shekinah.

Shekinah teaches us that God is as present on earth as in heaven. There is a divine embrace of all creation, of each of our lives and communities. It surrounds us like a morning mist, and while we may think it burns off when the heat is high in our lives, it does not. Someone once described Shekinah as the beautiful One who re-souls us when we are at the point of pain and helplessness.

Sometimes it can be hard to feel divine love when our lives are less than perfect. Still, the Spirit's love surrounds us with sweetness and power, whether we feel it or not. God's love is a part of us because the Spirit dwells within us, constantly looking for ways to support and free us. Love is who God is, and because of that, love is at the core of our own lives. It is as sure as sunrise — even more so.

Once, years ago, during a period of hardship in my life, I took some time away to write and reflect. To heal, really. To find some sense of warmth and direction. I went to a little cottage on the rocky coast of Nova Scotia. One morning, I was walking along the sandy beach when a dense fog rolled in. It seemed to come up quickly. It surrounded and disoriented me in seconds. For a moment, I panicked. I couldn't see my way home. So I just stood still and took deep breaths of the moist, salty air. I could hear the waves and the sea birds, but that was all.

Suddenly, I felt the fog itself become a kind of embrace, powerfully surrounding all of me, all the good and all the broken pieces of my heart and life. It felt like a divine hug, both tender and powerful. I knew then that all I needed to do to get to the cottage, and all I really needed to do in my life, was lean into that embrace and walk by the wild water until I found home. I knew, even though circumstances had not changed, that I was not alone in it all. God's Shekinah would never leave me.

From the Hebrew Scriptures we learn that God's Spirit is present on earth as a wild, fierce presence of creative love. This Spirit reaches out and embraces. It acts to bring life to life. It moves over the chaos of our lives and world, always looking for new starts. It is not about to be tamed by any words or human experience or expectation. The Spirit does not dominate, threaten, or coerce. The Spirit broods, creates, surrounds, dances, and liberates. After all, can any of us put a foot into the parted waters of the Red Sea in the hope of freedom without a little push from the Spirit?

GOD'S SPIRIT
IN THE NEW TESTAMENT

Much like *ruach* in the Hebrew Scriptures, the New Testament often uses the Greek word *pneuma* to represent the Spirit. Like *ruach*, it is the word for wind and breath. In addition, it describes the immaterial yet powerful essence of someone or something. It refers both to the Holy Spirit and to the inward being or personality of a person. In the New Testament, there is no cohesive doctrine of the Spirit. Sometimes the text speaks of the Spirit, the Holy Spirit, the Spirit of Christ, or the Spirit of God as if those terms are interchangeable. Perhaps in the mystery of the Trinity, they are. We can, however, begin to understand the presence of the Spirit in Jesus' words and the early believers' experiences.

In Jesus' passionate farewell to his followers in John 14:15–31, he promises his friends that, in the context of love and obedience, he will ask the Father to send the Spirit to help them after he is gone. He first describes the Spirit as "another Advocate" (v. 16). The Greek word, *parakleton,* can also be translated as Helper or Encourager. In Greek writings, this was the word for a legal adviser, one who pleads another's case or acts as a proxy. The use of the qualifier "another" helps us see that the Spirit is one who will continue the same awakening, loving, redeeming work of Jesus' earthly ministry. This is perhaps why the Spirit is sometimes referred to as the Spirit of Christ. Spirit as Advocate adheres to the truth, provides a defense (even if undeserved), and acts on behalf of the people. For the frightened disciples in that upper room long ago, the promise of a divine defense attorney must have been welcome news indeed!

The connotation of *parakleton* as Helper reminds us that, as we saw with Shekinah, we are never alone. Jesus expands that notion in verse 18 when he tenderly tells them that they will not be left "orphaned" and alone by the events that are about to unfold, even though Jesus will seem to be taken from them. This is a picture of the Spirit as adopter and rescuer.

About two years ago, my husband and I adopted a dog from a shelter nearby. Our beloved keeshond, Abigail, had died a few months earlier, and we were bereft. Our new dog, Bonnie, had known hard times. She had recently had puppies, and none of her puppies were found with her. When we went to pick her up, she was a wild thing. But we could feel the love in her. She bonded with us quickly, and now we cannot imagine our home without her. In a sense, we were Helper to her. In another sense, she was Helper to us. In that mutual adoption, we all experienced new grace.

Jesus is telling his friends that life in the Spirit will be similar to that, a mutual, loving, intimate relationship that changes everything, even deep grief. The Spirit comes, sees value, makes the case for our rescue, and then moves into the house with us.

Earlier, in verse 17, Jesus tells them more about the new Spirit that is on the way, "the Spirit of truth." The Greek word *aletheia* refers not so much to truth as opposed to a lie, as it does to "big truth," the truth that inhabits the very heart of things. It refers to the reality that is right before our eyes but sometimes out of sight at the same time. It is something that is actual, not counterfeit. It cannot be feigned. The *aletheia* that the Spirit insists on includes actual facts, of course, but also deeper realities. The Spirit of truth helps us by insisting that we confront our own blind spots or, at a bare minimum, acknowledge that they are there and that we do not know what we do not know. The Spirit of truth is an anti-arrogance potion. The Spirit desires that we examine our assumptions that hurt us and others. The Spirit insists that we take a look at the places in our lives where we function by rote so much that we regularly miss the wonder of the moment and our abundant daily opportunities for life and love.

Later in John 14, after Judas questions Jesus' plan, Jesus tells them all that the Spirit he will send will be both teacher and memory aid. It is the Spirit who opens our eyes to truth and teaches us the meaning and implications of God's ways and how we are to live them out in the world. Jesus goes so far as to say that the Spirit will *cause us* to remember what he has said (v. 26). By the very act of remembering, we awaken to the truth and embody it more perfectly.

One of the problems that humans face is that we live in a state of forgetfulness. We forget God and the power of God's ways. We forget our own identity as God's beloved children, so we don't treat ourselves or others as sacred vessels in which God dwells. The Spirit reawakens us to what is actually real and true, in and through us. The expression of Spirit truth will look different in each one of us, as we are uniquely chosen and shaped for just what we and the world most need to receive and to offer.

The Spirit, as our inner knower, does not disclose a truth that is foreign to us. It is within us, just as the Spirit is within us. We have simply grown apart, become estranged by inattention or distracted by a false flickering light that has been foisted on us by others we see as authoritative but who do not appreciate the truth. Even so, the Spirit gives us a questing spirit, a desire to arrive home again even if via a circuitous route. The Spirit inspires this kind of need in order to meet this kind of need. It is not certainty that meets our need for knowing. It is trust.

From the apostle Luke, in Acts 2:1–13 we get another glimpse into the Spirit's power and priorities. In this post-resurrection story, just after the disciples meet to discern the proper replacement for Judas, Peter and the others are gathered in Jerusalem when the heavens open and the Spirit descends on them like a rushing violent wind (as *ruach*) and settles on all those present as tongues of fire above each head. Fire, that profound biblical symbol for power and purification, does not descend as one great blanket of fire. It is individual. Each person receives the power and the cleansing that each so desperately needs in order to face the challenges and the wonders of post-resurrection life. Spirit fire also burns away injustice and division from them as a body. The text doesn't say that suddenly everyone speaks and understands Aramaic or Hebrew. It does not say that some new and heretofore unknown language is revealed. Rather, the text says that each understands what God is doing in his or her own language. No one language dominates. No one culture dominates. Each stands on its own and receives the truth and the refining of Spirit in the way that it can be understood.

Spirit fire still burns away illusions, half-truths, and arbitrary divisions. It is the equalizing power of the Spirit that allows no language or people to dominate but enables each to understand the other from their own sacred knowing. The Spirit does not choose sides. The Spirit actually breaks down entrenched positions and creates something entirely new. That breakdown is not one of destruction. The sides are not devalued or destroyed. They aren't even combined or melded. They are transformed, reconciled, united. A new thing has come.

Finally, I want to lift up one additional glimpse into the Spirit in the New Testament: the Spirit dwelling within us. For example, in Romans 8:9, the apostle assumes the indwelling presence of the Spirit as the ultimate guide and arbiter of faith and ethics. For Paul, we are not simply inhabited by the Spirit as if we could wall off the Spirit in a cupboard under the stairs and release power and insight only when comfortable or desperate. Rather, life and even our own bodies are infused with the One who is both wholly other and yet still one with us. With the understanding of the Spirit's indwelling, we no longer simply believe. We live and move and have our being experientially in Christ. Paul puts it this way: "It is no longer I who live, but it is Christ who lives in me" (Gal. 2:20). This amazing truth lies at the heart of my understanding of the fruit of the Spirit.

In Jesus' visitation with the disciples after the resurrection, he literally breathes the Spirit into them (John 20:22). Indwelling binds together the spiritual and physical in human life. What could be more incarnational than this? For reasons that boggle the mind, God chooses human bodies and human souls to manifest God's saving love in the world. From the moment Gabriel flutters into Mary's ordinary life with an outlandish action plan for the world, we have seen that the Spirit chooses human bodies to bring all that is needed into being. With Mary's powerful prayer, "Let it be with me according to your word" (Luke 1:38), she invites the Spirit into every corner of her life, every cell of her being. As a result, she is the one who brings Christ Jesus into the world. It is helpful to remember that the Spirit, while always present, working and helping, delivers bounty most lavishly when invited and welcomed.

Our roles in life and the cosmos are much less pivotal than Mary's, but they are no less Spirit imbued. The Spirit's presence within us gives a sacramental quality to all of life. Concrete objects and actions, by intention and grace, carry the Spirit's nurturing power into the experience of ordinary living. We then realize that the Spirit fills us with indwelling hope, an inner flow of happiness and aliveness that never fails even when we fail to notice.

TENDING SPIRIT

Paying attention to the Spirit within us can be dangerous. After all, what if we really open up and the Spirit wants something more from us than we are prepared to offer? I remember nights, now more than forty years ago, when I was wrestling with my call to ordained ministry. At the time, I had just graduated from college with a degree in creative writing and was working as a waitress at Joe Namath's restaurant in Tuscaloosa, Alabama. For some weeks, the Spirit woke me up in the night with an uneasiness and longing I couldn't tame. I did not want to be a minister. I wanted to live over some delicatessen in New York and wait in the cold, with open-fingered gloves and a ratty shawl, for my short stories to sell.

Finally, one night in my distress I found myself crying out, "O Lord, I don't want to be a minister. If I become a minister, I'll never get to wear my little black strapless cocktail dress again, and it is not even paid for!" I could almost hear the angels laughing. What I did not know then, and sometimes forget now, is that the Spirit knows me better than that. The Spirit knows you better than that. Known as we are, the Spirit knows what we need and when we need it. The Spirit will not offer us more than we are ready to receive, even of the Spirit's own presence or fruit. So there is no need to be fearful of what the Spirit offers or the cultivation of the Spirit's fruit. The Spirit recognizes that one perfect raspberry is enough to get us to the next one.

So, how do we recognize the Spirit's nudging, cajoling, or fierce fire in our lives? This is not often as easy as we think. Our egos have the wily ability to convince us that just about anything we want is what the Spirit wants for — or from — us. That is often not the case. Discernment is necessary to keep us from making ourselves into our own little gods and ascribing our wants to the Spirit.

What are we to do? First, we recognize the Spirit by what the Spirit does, especially deep inside us over time. Too often, mere transactions substitute for true transformation in our spiritual lives. We pray for healing, and healing comes. Then we put the Spirit back in the cupboard under the stairs until somebody else we love gets sick. Or we pray for a windfall, and it doesn't come. Then we say, "Thanks anyway," and proceed to try to get what we want by hook or by crook. The Spirit is not much interested in the merely transactional. The Spirit is interested in the transformational. So if you want to see the Spirit's handiwork in your life, look deeply within at the ways that you have changed for the better over time. See if you can see, in hindsight, the small steps toward that change. That is the Spirit's dance, and you can learn her steps.

A second great hint of the Spirit is surprise, or what seems like chance. An old friend calls just as you are remembering them, and you get a shimmery feeling of synchronicity and the sense that all of life is one piece of cloth. Experiences of connections and unity are the Spirit's language. If we stop and think about these moments, nine times out of ten, we will see something we've been blind to or realize something that needs our spiritual or physical attention that we have been ignoring.

A third thing we can look for is a sudden, unexpected feeling of homecoming and peace. That is often the Spirit's signal to stop and pay attention. There is something real and precious to be experienced in this moment. It is something to draw from and to tuck away for safekeeping. One of my former parishioners used to keep homing pigeons. Occasionally he was asked to bring them to graveside services. When he released them, there often was a collective gasp of apprehension (would they do as they had been taught?) and wonder as we watched them twirl, get their bearings, and head together toward what they knew to be home. In the Spirit, we are like that too. We may find ourselves in unfamiliar places, even grief-saturated places, but when we rise just a bit, the wind of the Spirit will always direct us toward home.

Finally, sometimes we have to learn a new language in order to discern the Spirit from ego. When we got our rescue dog, Bonnie, the first weeks were a wild exercise in cross-species communication. Frankly, she was better at it than we were. Eventually we learned that she responds best to both verbal cues and hand signals. It is the language that we have developed between us. Granted, sometimes it breaks down, but it is fairly reliable.

Each of us, as we delve into our relationship with the Spirit, will learn a new language of the heart. It may be a literal language, such as those who have the gift of tongues receive. For me, it is more a language of the heart that is formed by Scripture, experience, prayer, and the natural world. John Calvin said again and again that the two ways to know God are the Scriptures and the "theater of the creatures."[2] For him, there was no sure path, or even stability, apart from those two languages. Whatever language you find, it will be the language of the deepest possible communion, with all of its predictability and wondrous unexpectedness. The more we awaken to the language of Spirit, the more supple and moldable our souls, and even our structures, will be to new expressions of love that are right for our moment in history.

When it comes to the Spirit, sometimes the theological answers feel dry. How does a theologian explain "luminous"? How does a theologian explain a three-year-old seeing a bright, golden, dancing crown around her home? How does a theologian explain shimmering, unbelievable transformation without resorting to stale formulas? All we can do is stand with Mary Magdalene in stunned wonder in the garden of death's demise and hear the whisper in our own hearts, *"Rabbouni."*

WEEDING YOUR GARDEN

One of my favorite saints is Kateri Tekakwitha, a Mohawk Algonquin woman who is the patron saint of ecologists, the environment, and people in exile, all things close to my heart. What I love most about her, though, is her name. Tekakwitha means "she who bumps into things." I can so identify with that. Every day my ego trips me up, my habits make me tired, and my blinders and expectations lead me far away from the mark of a fruitful spiritual life.

Paul is well aware of this tendency as he writes to the Galatian church. Before he gives his description of the fruit of the Spirit, he paints a very different picture of an unbalanced, ego-saturated way of life that produces bitter fruit within the soul and the community. He lists fifteen specific manifestations of an ego-ruled life (Gal. 5:19–21). We each can compile our own list of stumblings. We know that we make choices that drip poison in our hearts and make it difficult to hear the Spirit or awaken to our own healing. Before you move to the next chapter, take some time to clear the ground of your soul a bit so that the insights you receive will not get choked out. Do this with honesty, humility, and a bit of detachment. Don't make excuses for what you see, but know that all is redeemable. Ask the Spirit to help you stand your ground emotionally as you seek to face your sin.

A WEEK FOR TENDING THE SPIRIT

These six daily Scriptures and reflections are designed to be used on Monday through Saturday, with Sunday being a time of worship with your community of faith. Or, if you are working through this book with a small group, you might want to start with Day One the day after your group meeting. Whatever pattern works for you is perfect.

Each day includes a Scripture reading to help you deepen your experience of the concepts in the chapter. I find benefit in doing my reflection in the morning and then returning to the Scripture at the close of day to see how the words have, or have not, informed my day. If you keep a journal, that is a great way to track this journey. I also find it helpful to write out the Scripture quotation in my own hand. This seems to give the words a deeper incarnational roost in me. You will quickly find what works best for you. Just be sure not to judge your practice against others, especially those in your small group. Harsh self-judgment is a powerful way to drown out the Spirit's voice. As Jesus says in the Beatitudes, you are blessed right now, not when you get your act together.

Day One: "When God began to create the heavens and the earth, the earth was complete chaos, and darkness covered the face of the deep, while a wind from God swept over the face of the waters" (Gen. 1:1–2). The word translated "wind" here is *ruach*. The Bible begins with the *ruach* of God sweeping over watery chaos and deep nothingness. What are the areas of chaos, darkness, or nothingness in your life, family, or world where you long to feel the Spirit sweeping, sorting, and bringing perfect light? How do you experience the Spirit in those areas of your life? Take a moment today to feel the wind on your face. Face into it if you can, and welcome the Spirit to sweep over your life.

Day Two: "The hand of the LORD came upon me, and he brought me out by the spirit of the LORD and set me down in the middle of a valley; it was full of bones" (Ezek. 37:1). Ezekiel's world is collapsing. All around him he sees destruction and decay, and he doesn't see a way out. In this powerful vision, God's Spirit assists him to face reality, to see the mess he and the people are in, how dire the situation is, and their inability to fix it on their own. For the Spirit to move to heal, it is often necessary that we face the real unvarnished truth of our lives. That is hard and sometimes painful, but it is the only way. Take a moment to think about any situations that seem dire and hopeless to you right now. How did it come to this? Tell the Spirit the truth. Don't be afraid to feel what you feel. Devastation never has the last word. If you find today that you feel helpless and hopeless, take a moment to stop and breathe the Spirit into those situations. Ask the Spirit, with hope in your heart, "Can these bones live?" Then listen to the answers.

Day Three: "Then he said to me, 'Prophesy to the breath, prophesy, mortal, and say to the breath: Thus says the Lord GOD: Come from the four winds, O breath, and breathe upon these slain, that they may live.' I prophesied as he commanded me, and the breath came into them, and they lived and stood on their feet, a vast multitude" (Ezek. 37:9–10). God commands Ezekiel to call on the power of the breath/Spirit (*ruach*) to repair the damage done. Ezekiel—unsure, no doubt—obeys, and the Spirit comes and brings that which was dead to life again. Are there areas of your life that feel old, dead, and dried up? What about your family? Community? How have the accumulations of sin left devastation around you? Within you? Pause for a moment. Notice what comes to your mind. Write about it if you choose. Ask the Spirit to breathe new life into you and the situations that come to mind. Today, set out to notice life signs in places where you usually don't expect to see them.

Day Four: "The angel said to her, 'The Holy Spirit will come upon you, and the power of the Most High will overshadow you; therefore the child to be born will be holy; he will be called Son of God'" (Luke 1:35). What follows this declaration is Mary's unequivocal yes. Let it be. What would it be like for you to say yes, let it be, today? How might God want the Spirit to empower you to be a God-bearer in your home, church, workplace, community? What would you need the Spirit to do for and in you in order for your witness to expand into a saving presence of love and freedom for those around you? Ask God to send you today just what you need. Try to notice those moments when you can bear Christ to others and bring saving love into their lives.

Day Five: "When he had said this, he breathed on them and said to them, 'Receive the Holy Spirit. If you forgive the sins of any, they are forgiven them; if you retain the sins of any, they are retained'" (John 20:22–23). In this resurrection appearance, Jesus breathes the Spirit into his disciples and connects the work of the Spirit within them specifically to forgiveness. For us, forgiveness is often not easy. We may long to do it and still feel unable to do so. If the wounds are deep enough, we may not even think forgiveness is justified. We might feel guilty that we can't do it. The Spirit can help. The Spirit longs for our release from bondage and knows that if we don't forgive, the emotional consequences can be dire. Are there any persons whom you want to forgive? Do you struggle to accept forgiveness for yourself? Why is that hard? Write about this if you choose. Think about what unforgiveness costs you. Ask the Spirit to help you see where forgiveness is needed and to strengthen you to begin. Don't be unforgiving of yourself if you can't do it. Sometimes forgiveness takes many, many breaths of the Spirit.

Day Six: "Therefore there is now no condemnation for those who are in Christ Jesus. For the law of the Spirit of life in Christ Jesus has set you free from the law of sin and of death" (Rom. 8:1–2). Paul is concerned about legalism killing people's souls and faith. Here he reminds us that the Spirit in us is always about setting us free from all that is death dealing. Are there areas of your life right now where you feel bound in unhealthy ways? Are you sometimes overcome with trying to do everything and do it all with excellence? If you close your eyes and imagine true freedom for your life, what does that include? Write about that. Now look at what you wrote. Is your dream consistent with what you know to be true about God and the values of God's ways? If yes, then ask for the Spirit's aid to lead you into freedom. If you are not sure, ask the Spirit to be your teacher and help you sort it all out. Today, try to notice moments when you feel truly and expansively free. Ask God to create a durable, free, and open space in your heart for the Spirit to grow a garden.

Questions for Reflection and Discussion

1. Ask the group to share their understanding of the Holy Spirit before they read this chapter. Did reading this chapter change anything in your understanding of the Spirit? If you could write a whole book on the Spirit, what would you include?
2. The chapter emphasizes that the Spirit cannot be fully understood or contained. Given that, what things help you understand the Spirit and how the Spirit works?
3. In this chapter, I share a childhood experience that I associate with the Spirit. Have you ever had a specific experience of the Spirit in your life that you would be willing to share?

4. This chapter offers a few hints for noticing the Spirit's activity in a person's life. What would you add to that list?
5. John Calvin talked about knowing God through the Scriptures and the "theater of the creatures." In what ways does nature help you experience the Spirit? How do you see the suffering of the Spirit in climate change, wildfires, deforestation, and the like? How might your group address some of these Spirit wounds?
6. What did you find most illuminating, meaningful, thought provoking, or disturbing in this chapter? Share your insights with the group.

CHAPTER 2

TENDING THE
SHOOTS OF LOVE

Love recognizes no barriers. It jumps hurdles,
leaps fences, penetrates walls to arrive at its
destination full of hope.

— Maya Angelou

A few years ago, as I sat cross-legged on my sofa, surrounded by books and yellow legal pads, researching
something now forgotten, I barely looked up as my husband, Robbie, went out to meet the UPS driver and then
tossed a small box in my lap. Then I saw the postmark. It
was from my best friend from the third grade, Harriett.
Harriett and her husband still live just around the corner
from the house in which I grew up.

Apparently, when Harriett was cleaning out a cupboard,
she came across a relic of mine. It was my "I love Paul" pin
from when I went to see the Beatles in concert in Atlanta
when I was eleven. She accompanied the now-corroded
pin with a simple note, "Those were the days." I smiled and
stopped in my tracks for a moment, remembering my love

of over fifty years for this friend, the sweet giddiness of a preteen's love for a rock star, and all the varied, wonderful, and confusing loves before and since.

The language of the Spirit's love is one with which we are largely less than fluent, no matter how many Hallmark movies we watch, how many "I love Paul" pins we keep, or how many moments of tender presence we experience. To try to define it is a bit like trying to nail smoke. We can feel its presence and be awed by its power, but we cannot define its parameters. It is essentially beyond us. But it is also within us. We are made from it. God is our only source of love and, like God, love will always remain a bit of a mystery. It is both the soil and the first blossom of the fruit of the Spirit. Without it, there will never be a harvest.

Teresa of Ávila calls love a science. There is indeed an alchemy about it. We can study it and explore it. We can experiment with it, but its true qualities emerge only over time and often quite unexpectedly. You never know exactly what you will get when you put the elements together.

Psychiatrist and theologian Gerald May talks about love as the irreducible energy at the core of every person, the base metal that animates us and makes us who we are. French Jesuit theologian Pierre Teilhard de Chardin claims that the very physical structure of the universe is love. In all its orbits, bursts, contractions, brilliance, and empty spaces, it is all love doing its thing. The apostle John writes it even more simply, "Whoever does not love does not know God, for God is love" (1 John 4:8).

LOVE IN THE BIBLE

The Scriptures create a beautiful mosaic of the scope and complexity of human love, God's love for humankind, and the created order. Scripture itself can be seen as the testimony of a great love, filled with passionate embraces, painful breakups, and joyous reunions.

In the Hebrew Scriptures, love (*'ahavah*) is an all-encompassing word that, depending on the context, can mean anything from deep passion with a strong emotional attachment that desires to possess or to be in the presence of the beloved, to familial love, or even friendship. In each instance, it is a strong attachment with an equally strong commitment.

In the Greek language of the New Testament, several different words for love were in common usage at the time of Jesus. Two of those do not appear in the New Testament explicitly. One is *eros*, which refers to passionate love that desires to become one with the beloved. *Eros* is the type of love that predominates in the Song of Solomon to describe both human passion and the passion between God and the soul. While the second word, *storge* (signifying affection, as between parents and children), is also not found in the New Testament, its opposite (*astorgos*) appears twice: in Romans 1:31 to describe those who are hard-hearted and have no tender affection and in 2 Timothy 3:3 to describe a heartless generation. In Romans 12:10, *storge* is combined with another Greek word for love, *phileo*, to form *philostorgos*, which means loving dearly, being devoted and affectionate. *Phileo* is used frequently in the New Testament and refers to the warm love we feel for those who are our nearest and dearest. It is the word that most accurately describes the feelings of love that wash over us from time to time in families and close friendships. It is what I felt when I opened Harriett's box and felt the flood of memories that came with it. *Phileo* is often what we mean when we talk about loving God. It refers to tenderness and the sturdy emotional bond between people that can express itself in dedication and acts of kindness.

The word for love that occurs most often in the New Testament, nearly three hundred times, is *agape*. This word was not in common usage in Jesus' day. It was considered an antique word that had dropped from people's everyday vocabulary. Jesus' followers, and the early evangelists, took it up and specialized it to describe the life-changing love of God for us in Jesus Christ. It became the hallmark of relationship with God and our interactions with others.

Agape is often defined as unconditional love. I define it as unconquerable love. *Agape* cannot be stopped by anything that the beloved does or does not do. It is love that always seeks the highest good for the other. *Agape* is not so much a category of the heart as it is an ethic, a category of the will. While other kinds of love sweep into our hearts, often unbidden, *agape* is something that one chooses. *Agape* is an unshakable orientation toward others and the world that insists on doing the best for the beloved. *Agape* can certainly be accompanied by strong emotions. It is just not dependent on them or tethered to them. It is righteousness in action. It summons healing, growth, and perfection in the other. It is, as God's love always is, endlessly creative, finding a way when there is no way, making something wonderful from nothing at all. This is the kind of love that Jesus can command and expect of us toward even our enemies, when what we feel for them may be anything but loving.

We cannot always love on a feeling level, but we can always allow the Spirit's *agape* to operate in us. We can exercise *agape* like a muscle. Often feelings of love will follow our choices to love—not always, but given enough time, often. Even if warm feelings do not follow, that does not release us from the call to love even if it seems impossible. God does not command the impossible, because as Spirit-indwelt beings, *agape* is always possible. The maturing of *agape* happens slowly over time through continued intimacy with God, not a dogged personal discipline. The Spirit in us gradually brings *agape* to maturity in the context of family and community and releases the powerful and tender qualities of love in our lives and world.

Paul uses the word *agape* to begin his description of Spirit-matured life in Galatians 5:22 because all the aspects of the fruit flow from it. It is *agape* breaking out in human experience and relationships that is the catalyst for real transformation of soul, community, and creation. Perhaps Paul places love first on the list not just because it is primary but because it needs the most time. Once it pokes through the soil of the soul, though, the garden seems to diversify and flourish at a breakneck pace.

When we open to *agape* and allow it to flow through us, then it is not really our love at all. It is the Spirit loving in and through us. Self-centeredness dissolves, and we are pure conduit. We awaken to what we always are, even when unaware, the hands, feet, and hearts of God loving the world into wholeness.

QUALITIES OF *AGAPE*

While a concise definition of *agape* that covers its scope and nuances is impossible, the Scriptures point us to aspects that allow us to recognize *agape* at work in our lives and communities. In Paul's first letter to the church in Corinth, a church struggling mightily with relationships, he offers a soaring picture of the distinctives of Spirit love in human relationships.

In 1 Corinthians 13, often called the love chapter, he gives his friends hallmarks by which they can evaluate their own love walks. Several of the words he uses (*patient, kind, faithful*) are aspects of the fruit that we will examine in detail in later chapters. In verses 4–6, Paul tells us in essence that *agape* tames the ego. His word choices are evocative and humbling.

He tells us that *agape* is not jealous. The word he uses is a word for zeal that stakes a possessive claim on someone and something. It is a passionate word that, in some contexts, is seen as a positive quality. Here, though, Paul seems to point out that *agape* has at its heart a quality of releasing the beloved from claims that might harm. It protects us from the damage that can be done to self and others when we are clingy or feel threatened. *Agape* releases and doesn't cling. Why? Because *agape* is Spirit love working through us, and the Spirit is not clingy or needy.

Paul goes on to tell his friends that *agape* demonstrates a number of outward behaviors and doesn't demonstrate others. The word we translate as "rude" literally means to behave disgracefully or obnoxiously. *Agape* does not allow its own momentary needs or fears to become an excuse to behave obnoxiously toward others who may threaten or from whom we seek some kind of return. *Agape* doesn't seek to win at all costs, become boastful, become easily irritated, or keep score of wrongs. This is staggeringly countercultural for many of us. Still, as *agape* matures in us, we feel a new kind of lightness to life, even in its heaviest moments. We learn that we cannot always tell who is winning by the score and that the only thing that truly matters is the path toward spiritual maturity, not picayune irritations and scoring points. Without that lightness, life can become one long wasteland of disappointments and grievance.

I once had a parishioner who kept a spiral notebook of every grievance she had with me, the church, and its members. The burden of carrying those grievances eventually made her participation in the church impossible. She could not love any of us, nor could she receive the considerable love that we had to offer her. As she left our fellowship, she felt compelled to go over the notebook's contents with me, including some slights going back twenty years. It was one of the saddest conversations I have ever been a part of. Both of our egos were fully engaged, and all I wanted was for it to be over. We drew out the worst in each other, and therefore truly wishing each other well, which is a hallmark of *agape*, eluded us both. Months later when her new pastor called me, asking for help, I confess to a bit of schadenfreude. I rejoiced secretly that he was dealing with what I had dealt with. That is exactly what Paul says *agape* does not do. *Agape* does not rejoice in wrongs but rejoices in the truth.

Truth is the soil in which *agape* finds its deepest joy. It cannot grow strong in an environment in which truth is relative, whitewashed, or manipulated. When we accept lies as truth, or even insist that our experience is the sum total of all truth, then it is hard to choose the good for another whose experience, priorities, or ideology is different. When *agape* begins to mature, it softens the hard and judgmental tendencies of the soul. That does not mean that we compromise core beliefs. It simply means that we find we are able to love beyond them without requiring others to agree or adhere to our standards. That, too, has a taming effect on the ego.

In addition to taming our egos and helping us consider our motivations, Paul tells us that love is durable. "It bears all things, believes all things, hopes all things, endures all things" (v. 7). The phrase we translate as "bears all things" literally means "covers all things." In other words, *agape* "covers a multitude of sins" (1 Pet. 4:8). It outlasts even the worst that human beings can do to one another. Affection and passion may not have the same staying power, but *agape* cannot be destroyed by either hardship, hate, or the desire for retaliation. This stands to reason because it is the very nature and substance of God, whose love for us is not diminished by our response to that love or inability to live out of it consistently. God's love never fails nor ends; it is always available for us to dip back into even when our own capacities seem depleted.

Love is God's answer to fear. In 1 John 4:18, the writer tells us that "there is no fear in love, but perfect love casts out fear." In Scripture, "fear" does not simply refer to feelings of terror that sometimes overwhelm us. Rather it refers to our response to terror—the turning and running that seem so natural when we are threatened. In saying that perfect (or completed) love "casts out fear," John says simply that love doesn't run. In Ephesians 6, the author gives a list of "the whole armor of God" that is available to meet the challenges of life. Even though such armor existed at that time, the list names no armor for the back side of the body, because apparently one wearing God's armor never turns and runs.

That sounds lovely, but fear is still real in many of our lives on a near daily basis. We fear losing our jobs, or a horrible diagnosis, or the death of a loved one, or a wily microbe that could kill us. We fear war and violence. We fear what we do not know, what we cannot understand, and what threatens our worldview and the comfort zones we have crafted to get through the day. In the real lives that we live, how does *agape* cast out fear?

In my experience, *agape* does not always stop the feelings of fear or anxiety that are a part of everyday life in a complex world. What *agape* does is help me see, especially as I look at the life of Jesus, a pathway and partner through fear. When bombs fall, literally or metaphorically, it is the partnership with Jesus and the presence of the Spirit in all her loving vastness that gets me through. When I recently sat thunderstruck before images of the attack on Israel and the carnage of escalating war, I found myself immobilized. My outrage at the brutality overwhelmed me. I had no place to put it all. So I went out on my deck for a few moments, sat in the sunshine, breathed as deeply as I could through my sobs, and sat with God's broken heart. We grieved together. We sat shivah together. In that moment, *agape* found a way to break through. It did not change the circumstances or my grief or helplessness, but it did somehow mysteriously shift and change my fear. The love of God was big enough for me, and it changed me. Granted, my loved ones are not being tortured and killed. I don't know what it would be like then. But in that soft moment, God's *agape*, God's never-failing desire to choose the good for all, softened the edges of my fear, and fear loosened its grip on my heart.

Agape takes risks and makes sacrifices. For Christians, the most reliable model for how to live the life of *agape* is the incarnation of Jesus and his life, death, and resurrection. In the Jesus story, we learn how to tend love in our own simple lives. From Jesus, we learn that *agape* cannot be contained in the heart of God. It overflows. It bursts forth. It calls out evil and hypocrisy. It heals. It points the way, sweeps the path, defies the odds. It never gives up. It casts out fear, and it never ends. Love has already won.

Sometimes, as it did in Jesus' life, *agape* leads to pain. Maybe the balance tips to joy, contentment, and determination most of the time, but not all the time. Sometimes we lose the ones we love, and that pain sears with such exquisite breathless agony that we think that love is actually a demon, a cruelty. But deep in the ground of the Spirit's garden in our souls, we know, even then, that it is not. *Agape* is the force of the Force. It is what actually binds the human family together. It is nothing more or less than the reality of the essence of God. So even our tears water the garden, just as Jesus' did before the tomb of his dear friend Lazarus, or while he wept so hard in the Garden of Gethsemane that he bled.

Agape is stronger than pain or death. It is also more complicated. There is a vulnerability that is part and parcel of love. That is also true for God. When God chooses to love us, God also becomes open to our rejection. When Jesus in flesh chose to love us, he became vulnerable to the worst that human beings can do to one another. To awaken to the power of *agape* is also to accept the pain of it. Not all those to whom we give ourselves will want that gift. Not all those for whom we seek the good will accept, or even recognize, the good when it is offered. *Agape* chooses to do it anyway.

OBJECTS OF LOVE
AND WEEDS IN THE GARDEN

When asked which of God's values was to hold first priority for believers, Jesus replied with what we call the Summary of the Law. "The first is, 'Hear, O Israel: the Lord our God, the Lord is one; you shall love the Lord your God with all your heart and with all your soul and with all your mind and with all your strength.' The second is this, 'You shall love your neighbor as yourself.' There is no other commandment greater than these" (Mark 12:29–31). This profound expression of the primacy of love, drawn from Deuteronomy 6:4–5 and Leviticus 19:18, gives us the scope of love's power and range. Scholars debate the exact meaning of the text. Who is included in "neighbor"? What does love of self look like? Wherever we land in that discussion, what is clear is that love always has an object. It is concrete and never abstract. It is revealed not simply in the heart but in specific action for the good.

Love of God and the Weed of Violence

As I watched images from the brutal war in Israel and Palestine flood my TV screen, I was struck by a phrase that one of the reporters used. In speaking of the sounds of the bombs falling and sirens wailing, she said that it would be the soundtrack of their lives for the foreseeable future. I thought of my own experience with bomb blasts, which I share in chapter 5, and shuddered yet again at the choices that human beings sometimes make that do violence to God by harming fellow humans made in God's image.

Violence in any form is incompatible with *agape*'s growth and maturing. At the heart of the Ten Commandments is God's rock-solid value that we are not to kill, damage, or disrespect others. We cannot put God first and love God as our one and only while simultaneously engaging in violence to solve our problems, address our rage, reduce our anxiety, or somehow maintain our security.

Still, we always find reasons for violence. It can even seem unavoidable, reasonable, and justified. Sometimes the weeds that strangle *agape* are disguised as good and necessary. That makes them hard to identify and difficult to uproot. Sometimes competing allegiances, customs, and values make violence seem a natural and laudatory mode for self-defense. Sometimes, even indwelt by the Spirit, we feel forced to make choices between worse and worst more often than between better and best. Sometimes we are caught between a rock and a hard place, and none of the available choices seem good and loving. When those times arise, and circumstances larger than ourselves seem to make our decisions for us, all we can do is confess and sit with God as God grieves the loss of God's own children and humanity's inability to be regularly transformed by *agape* in the arenas of power. In moments like those, pulling the weed of violence and not allowing it to propagate even in our own hearts, sitting and mourning with God, confessing honestly personal and communal failure and sin, is a powerful outpouring of our love toward God. When we have the courage and humility to look at the hard things without turning back or turning away, we show our love to God. In return, the Spirit begins to sow new depths of love in our hearts that gradually open new questions and new solutions to even age-old conundrums.

Love of Neighbor and the Weed of Injustice

Love of God is, by definition, also expressed toward our neighbors. We begin to do that with the recognition that *agape* cannot grow in the soil of injustice. When we separate love from justice, it becomes, at best, mere sentimentality and, at worst, nothing more than Narcissus at the pool seeing only himself reflected in the water. When we decide we are willing for *agape* to emerge as a force in our lives, we immediately move against any form of domination or injustice. Just as Jesus tells us that he and the Father are one, love and justice are also one. They may seem to function differently at times, but they cannot be untangled.

Biblical justice is *agape*'s action plan in community. Justice in the Bible is not about people getting what we think they deserve. It is not about putting wrongdoers behind bars as an end in itself. It is not about balancing scales that cannot be balanced by mandating harm for harm. It is not retaliation, and it has no violence or revenge in it. Justice is the work of ensuring that all of God's children, and the entire created order, are free to become all that God has dreamed for them to be. Love of neighbor seeks to ensure that no impediments, especially the systemic weeds of prejudice, hate, and power, are allowed to deny persons what is needed for a life of dignity and fullness. *Agape* can exist in human community only in the context of that freedom and inclusion.

Jesus consistently widens our lens of who falls within the scope of the Spirit's injustice-eradicating love. He uses a despised Samaritan to show us what *agape* looks like in daily life (Luke 10:25–37). He chooses an outcast, broken-hearted Samaritan woman he meets at a well to be his first messenger of forgiving love to her community (John 4). He is even persuaded in a feisty argument with a Syro-phoenician woman who is seeking help for her child that love is not reserved for only some (Mark 7:24-30). He erases strict gender roles by teaching women along with men (Luke 10:39) and reveals his resurrected self first to women who were considered so untrustworthy that they were not allowed to testify in a court of law. What is clear in these and many other stories is that, in Christ, divisions of prejudice and hierarchical oppression are reduced to dust.

Still, in Jesus' day, and certainly in our own, those divisions remain. We, too, can find ourselves arguing about who is worthy of love, who is worthy of inclusion, who it is acceptable to love and seek the good for. Those arguments may be evil's favorite food. They inevitably lead to an us-versus-them mentality that descends quickly into hate in its many disguises. Humans have the terrible tendency to become what we love, even if what we love is hate.

While the opposite of *phileo* might be apathy, the opposite of *agape* is oppression. The wily thing is that even when we choose oppression and make enemies, the Scripture does not allow us a free pass from loving them. Jesus in his seminal Sermon on the Mount makes that explicit. "You have heard that it was said, 'You shall love your neighbor and hate your enemy.' But I say to you: Love your enemies and pray for those who persecute you, so that you may be children of your Father in heaven, for he makes his sun rise on the evil and on the good and sends rain on the righteous and on the unrighteous" (Matt. 5:43–45). There is much to unpack in those verses. For our purposes, what is clear is that if we want to live as God's children, that is, people who look like God and carry God's name, then our *agape* cannot be reserved for those we like and with whom we agree.

This is difficult, to be sure. Often we need moments to step back and regroup in order to drink from the Spirit's well of love so that we have resources to strengthen love's resolve in our daily choices and long-term goals. Sometimes we need to distract ourselves briefly from the difficulty of concretely loving our neighbors, but we cannot allow confusion or overwhelm to set our agenda for long. The bottom line is that we cannot work for the good of neighbor while simultaneously supporting or denying oppression. When we try to do that, even with elaborate excuses, everything we touch is tainted. People become objects, like Horcruxes in *Harry Potter,* in which we deposit fragments of our shattered, fear-drenched souls. *Agape* is something that we must continually choose so that we do not lose the will to do the hard work of justice.

Love of Self and the Weed of Self-Hate

If *agape* is not flowing naturally to neighbors without condition or expectation of return, the problem is often that we are unable to love ourselves in a healthy way. People who inwardly despise themselves, especially if that animosity is unacknowledged or covered up with bravado, will usually project that animosity outward onto others. "They" become the problem that explains our negative emotions, fears, or real-life problems. "They" then must be suppressed. "They" are why we are unhappy and dissatisfied and always feel threatened. When "they" are dealt with, removed, or kept in their place, then everything will be as we dream it to be. This is, of course, the opposite of the truth. Our stunted selves are the problem. But we don't see that, so we put the energy that could go into love into stamping down what is true in favor of masks, slogans, and the ultimate fruit stunter — creating enemies instead of neighbors.

Mature self-love can be a challenge. Once in a particularly difficult time in my life, I was sitting on my sofa talking to a friend whom I trusted. In the course of telling her what was happening, I started blaming myself for everything, criticizing my every action and motivation. After I had been at that a while, and a bit of my pain energy was spent, she touched me on my shoulder and said, "Stop being so mean to my friend!" It took my breath away in that moment to realize how easily the "as yourself" part of the great love commandment eludes me.

In looking at the Summary of the Law, we may wonder, was Jesus fearful that we loved ourselves too much and that we needed to up our game with our neighbors? I can see that. Or was the command really for three loves in order of primacy: God first, then neighbor, and self following behind? As is true with so much of Scripture, the Spirit guides us to hear in the words exactly what each of our souls needs most. If we are not sure about God, the passage calls us to try loving God anyway. If we are harsh and judgmental of neighbors and always making excuses for our own behavior, we are invited to look at that. And if we wouldn't dare treat others with the same disdain with which we often treat ourselves, the text calls us to make a change. Obviously, love of God, neighbor, and self are not three separate loves from which to choose the easiest and most palatable.

Applying the standard of always choosing the good for ourselves can be daunting. As an only child, I was always cautioned against being selfish. From a young age, I tried not to take up too much space in a room, talk too much, or laugh too loud. I was royally unsuccessful at this. Nevertheless, the scroll runs under my life to this day, *don't be selfish*. Obviously, loving self and being selfish are two different things. Being selfish emerges from pain, from fear, or sometimes from a desire to hide shame. Healthy self-love arises from the soil of grace and forgiveness.

None of us has lived our lives perfectly. If we have made more than a handful of trips around the sun, we have accumulated enough failures and missteps to begin to color our sense of self. If our failures were mismanaged as children, or neurotically magnified as adults, we can quickly find it hard to love ourselves well. We are always too fat, too skinny, too pimply faced, too slow-witted, or too rejectable. And it is all our fault because we are somehow defective. Then the natural, and sometimes deserved, guilt we feel when we do something bad or cause another harm morphs into shame not for what we have done but for who we are. This shame can permeate the heart. We often have no words to describe it. There is just a relentless feeling that we are somehow less than whole, less than worthy of love. When that happens, we can strangle the tender shoots of love that constantly arise from Spirit because they don't look like the flower we think we and others would prefer.

I have often wondered if, when Jesus asks us to love our enemies, we must begin with our inner enemy. The twentieth-century psychiatrist Carl Jung says that the essential work of becoming a transformed self includes facing and embracing our shadow side. The shadow is the often unconscious yet powerful pattern of the unique frailties of our characters, our hurtful impulses, and our brokenhearted fears.

When I was in seminary, I was haunted by a frightening, recurring dream. I dreamed that I had been chased into the woods and was hiding for my life. I crouched behind a boulder and peeped around to see a group of terrifying people/monsters. They were painted like the demons in Dante's *Inferno* and carried fierce swords and pitchforks.

They were dancing around a fire celebrating that they would roast and eat me. I always woke up in a sweat, certain that I was not enough to face the monsters that were out to get me.

Finally, I talked to my spiritual director about this dream. He advised me that if the dream occurred again, I should simply step from behind the boulder and ask the monsters for their names and what they needed. Sure enough, in a few days, the dream returned. Somehow, I willed myself to come out from behind the stone and approach them. I asked each for his name. Each named a memory that I was ashamed of or a character flaw that I feared. I asked the name of the fire. It was Defective. Then I asked what they wanted. They said in unison, "We just want to come with you." Then they began to cry, and their tears put out the fire. I never had the dream again.

What I learned from it, with a good bit of help, was that until we can see ourselves with a measure of clarity, face our faults, and accept the love of God that makes us whole, wastes nothing, and produces fruit even from weed-infested ground, we will always look for ways out of pain and loneliness that often strangle both tender love and ethical love in our lives. We can't stay behind the boulder and march in the light of God's love at the same time. God's love and our own tender shoots of love always call forth what is truest in us. We may stumble and trip on brambles of neediness or subterranean wounds, but the Spirit's loving goal is always to mature us into the selves we were created to be.

In our tending of Spirit's garden, facing our shadow helps us develop a healthy love of self that allows us to awaken to God as both the great energy that spangles the heavens and the most intimate lover of our souls. That bud grows into the capacity to love God, neighbor, and self with freedom, courage, and purpose.

CONCLUSION

In a nutshell, Paul tells us, and Jesus shows us, that *agape* can hold all things, handle all things, and face all things. Paul reminds us that no matter how mature we become, we will always see the scope of love dimly, as in a poor-quality mirror. Even so, it is the greatest aspect of human life. It can withstand anything, even our worst fears, even death itself. Love never fails. It cannot fail, because it is God. Even if love seems to elude us, it is ever available and within us. Knowing that love is not something we must seek, but rather is already personally present, can help us assess our own loving actions. As at an annual appointment with the doctor, we can ask: Is the love we offer durable, like God's love for us? Is it sturdy, patient, kind, accepting? Do we reflect God's sturdy, patient, and kind love received in the way we share love? Are there weeds of impatience, violence, injustice, and self-hatred that need to be addressed? Love is both the evaluation and the cure.

The power of God's love moving through human agents can change things. It may not stop the storms. It may not explain away our fears, but it changes our experience of what we are going through. *Agape* has the power to quiet the thunders of the heart and maybe even the thunders of the world. It is good medicine. It doesn't always arrive with predictable miracles, at least not in my experience. The sturdy, calming medicine of God's love, more often than not, comes to us in the moments we need it most through the ones who have tended its garden most dependably. Song of Solomon 8:6 tells us that "love is strong as death." The resurrection of Jesus tells us that it is far stronger than that. "It bears all things, believes all things, hopes all things, endures all things" (1 Cor. 13:7) and never fails. God's constant choosing the good for us never ends.

A WEEK FOR TENDING LOVE

Day One: "You shall not take vengeance or bear a grudge against any of your people, but you shall love your neighbor as yourself: I am the LORD" (Lev. 19:18). Think today about any people toward whom you have hard or negative feelings. Who tends to irritate you? Whom do you avoid? Why do they get to you? What can they teach you? What is their gift to you? Take a moment to close your eyes and visualize them (if it is not too painful). Pray love and forgiveness into their lives. You don't have to initiate contact. It is enough to send love in your heart.

Day Two: "Whoever loves father or mother more than me is not worthy of me, and whoever loves son or daughter more than me is not worthy of me, and whoever does not take up the cross and follow me is not worthy of me" (Matt. 10:37–38). This is one of Jesus' hard sayings! He is not saying that we are not to love our families deeply, even above all earthly things. But whatever we love most will, in the final analysis, rule our lives. How can you love your family rightly this week? What opportunities might you have today to show your love for Jesus and to make your relationship with him your priority? Take time today to thank God for those whom you love. Make an appointment with Jesus in prayer and tell him how important he is to you.

Day Three: "I give you a new commandment, that you love one another. Just as I have loved you, you also should love one another" (John 13:34). Jesus loved us selflessly, compassionately, with understanding and forgiveness. In what ways do those characteristics mark your relationships? When you look at your life, who is included in the "one another"? Who is excluded? Why? Take a moment to close your eyes and let the faces of all the people in your life come into your mind's eye. Thank God for the many loves in your life and ask Jesus to help you love in the same way he does.

Day Four: "Let love be genuine; hate what is evil; hold fast to what is good; love one another with mutual affection; outdo one another in showing honor" (Rom. 12:9–10). Sometimes we think that the love of other people must be a deep emotional feeling. For that reason, we think that we cannot genuinely love if we do not "feel" loving. On the contrary, love is a choice. To love genuinely is to choose to do the best for the other. Often when we choose to love, loving feelings catch up with us. Think today of people for whom you can do a loving act. Perhaps it is as small as helping with a household chore or sending a note of thanks for kindness. Rehearse in your mind all the good qualities of each of the people in your life. Think of the tender ordinary moments and give thanks to God for those whom you love.

Day Five: Read 1 Corinthians 13 in your own Bible. Make a list of each of the qualities of love that Paul outlines in this beautiful poem. Ask yourself to what extent these qualities are obvious in your life with those closest to you. With your acquaintances? With your church family? In your community? As you prayerfully read the chapter, ask the Holy Spirit to inspire you in your love walk. Ask the Spirit to give you special insight into the ways and character of Christian love. You might want to read the passage over three times and come back to it during the day. Make a commitment today to bring love to mind throughout the day and to try to express love in all that you do.

Day Six: "So we have known and believe the love that God has for us. God is love, and those who abide in love abide in God" (1 John 4:16). The essence and nature of God is love. God is not sentimental or overly permissive. God simply chooses the best for us, at every moment in every circumstance. God is brimming with compassion, delight, and forgiveness. How might you make your day a more love-filled one? How can you abide in God's love today? Are there worries, feelings of inadequacy, or guilt that you need to get rid of? Send them off on the great stream of God's love as if they were tiny boats made of leaves. Whenever your mind wanders today, draw it back to God's love for you. Stop for a moment and feel the sweet truth of your life: you are God's delight, God's pride and joy, God's reason for salvation. Thank God for that great love that frees you. Ask God to mold you into a person whose primary characteristic is love.

Questions for Reflection and Discussion

1. Discuss how you understand the differences between *eros*, *phileo*, *storge*, and *agape*. Can you think of examples of each type of love in your experience? How do they interrelate? Do you think there is any such thing as false love? What might be a better word for that?

2. Feelings of love are glorious. They can also be deceptive. Can you think of a time when you thought you were experiencing love but it was not that? Can you think of examples of how the word "love" is misused in our culture?

3. Augustine once said, "Love God and do as you will." What do you think he meant by that?

4. Many of the ancient spiritual writers talk about choosing the path of love as a way to lighten the sorrow of God. How do you respond to that idea? Can you think of a time when love lightened your sorrow?

5. *Agape* disintegrates divisions but not boundaries. What are the qualities of healthy boundaries in our loving?

Can you think of a time when those boundaries got murky? What was the result?

6. Teilhard de Chardin once said that if we could harness the energy of love we would discover fire. How do you think the energy of love can burn away injustice, prejudice, and oppression? How specifically can *agape* work for the good in your circumstances and community? What would that look like?

CHAPTER 3

TENDING THE
SHOOTS OF JOY

Joy is the infallible sign of the presence of God.
—Pierre Teilhard de Chardin

Years back, I served for a short time as interim pastor of a small church in the Colorado high country. The church was a federation of a United Methodist congregation and a Presbyterian Church (U.S.A.) one. Most Sundays we met in the little Presbyterian building on the corner because it had a newly renovated fellowship hall that was perfect for Sunday school and snacks after the service. But on Christmas Eve, we met at the United Methodist building on the other end of the block. Christmas Eve that year was bitterly cold with light snow swirling around the lampposts decked with wreaths and red bows. In the sanctuary, the Chrismon tree was decorated and awaiting the signal to turn on the lights at the most dramatic moment. Poinsettias banked the Communion rail. The elements for the sacrament were on the table in finely polished silver vessels used only on Christmas Eve.

All was in order. Or so I thought until I started counting out the little candles to be lit at the close of the service. We didn't have enough. So I dutifully donned hat, coat, boots, and gloves to walk the half block to the small general store that I knew kept a supply of candles for use during blizzard blackouts. The sun was setting and rimmed the mountains with the look of fire. Snow was deepening, and there was a dreamy quality to the scene for this southern girl who more often wore a T-shirt for Christmas than a Fair Isle sweater.

When I entered the little store with its well-worn wooden floors and crowded shelving, the steam from the heat fogged up my glasses. As I stopped near the door to clean them, I saw a young mother pushing a double stroller. She was having trouble maneuvering, so I held the door for her, commenting on her young twins. They could not have been more than a month old. Each was dressed in a little white snowsuit that matched the mom's jacket. One suit was embroidered in golden threads with the simple word "Hope" surrounded by little snowflakes. The other was similar, with the word "Joy." I commented on how appropriate those were for Christmas Eve. The mom looked at me with glittering love-struck eyes and said, "Oh, no. Those are the girls' names. Aren't they beautiful?" Indeed they were.

I have often thought of that cold Christmas Eve in that little community where we shuffled through the snow to celebrate hope realized and the exquisite joy of the incarnation. Just the memory of it opens up my heart a little and I once again feel the sweet joy of God that too often lies dormant in my heart.

JOY IN THE BIBLE

The word that Paul chooses to describe Spirit joy is vast and nuanced. It can mean anything from wild hilarity to calm pleasure, and everything in between. It is used to describe a feeling of delight, gladness, contentedness, or mirth. Sometimes it is used to describe the feeling one has when one recognizes grace or when one receives some kind of benefit. It is used to describe the feeling of relief that comes when dire circumstances shift for the better. It is used to describe the wonderment of inner release when our burdens are removed by grace or forgiveness. It is a feeling that is associated with cooperating with God, with knowing God's will and doing it with assurance.

It is natural that Paul moves directly from Spirit love to Spirit joy in order to help believers understand what their lives are intended to look like and produce. Love and joy cannot be separated. Joy is the result of a deep conviction that, no matter what, God and life are good. Joy is rooted in God's love and our trust that in God we are headed in a good direction. Joy is rooted in our belief that we are already living in eternity.

We discover early on in the Christ story that the purpose of the incarnation is joy. "See, I am bringing you good news of great joy for all the people: to you is born this day in the city of David a Savior, who is the Messiah, the Lord" (Luke 2:10–11). We are used to saying that the life of faith is all about grace, all about love. And it is. It is also all about joy. Joy is the currency of the universe itself and, as the Westminster Catechism tells us, is the chief purpose of our lives. Joy is why Jesus was born (at least in part), and joy is why we were born as well so that we can love and enjoy God forever. This kind of enjoyment of God always ushers in praise and wonder that allows us to see God's glorious hand in even small moments.

Joy is also the feeling of centeredness and expansiveness that can arise even when circumstances are difficult. Last December I had a tough day of making the five-hour round-trip drive from our holiday home to Mobile, Alabama, for doctors' appointments that included an MRI. I am a little claustrophobic and was anxious about spending an hour in that little MRI tube. The technicians were very kind. They gave me a panic button to push if I truly couldn't cope and put earphones on me through which they played a Christmas music radio station. The songs were mostly secular, "White Christmas," "Frosty the Snowman," and the like. However, when I was so uncomfortable that I was about to push the button, the station played "Angels We Have Heard on High." My favorite. I found that even in my discomfort, the beauty of that well-loved hymn settled me. I found myself smiling. Did I still hate that tube? Yes. Was I still in pain? Yes. But something larger than that was released. The discomfort was no longer front of mind. Angels singing praises to God was front of mind. Beneath my circumstances I felt a calm joy that was bigger than anything else.

Joy often arrives when something wonderful pierces fear. Joy is what the Spirit produces in us because it is who the Spirit is. For that reason, joy is independent of circumstances and can be accessed in any situation at any time.

That may be hard to accept, especially when we confuse joy with happiness or getting what we think that we want. Happiness is usually linked to what happens to us from the outside. If a project goes well, or the family reunion is free from rancor, or the test results come back clear, or the prize patrol catches us in our ratty bathrobe and hands us a check for $10 million, we feel happy. Things are going well, so happiness seems warranted.

Joy is bigger and deeper than happiness. It is wilder, and it can be wilier. It can, on occasion, release happiness in us, but not all the time. Joy bubbles up from a deep root that cannot be shaken and recognizes that all is well, even when we are not happy and things do not seem to be, or truly are not, going well at all. That deep root which "knows" that all is well may sometimes be hard to access.

Still, it is there, and when we stop to look for it, it can change our feelings about just about anything.

JOY AND SUFFERING

In the year 203 CE, a high-born and high-spirited young Roman noblewoman living in the Mediterranean coastal town of Carthage in North Africa was martyred for her Christian faith. Her name was Perpetua. She was a young mother who was put to death along with her servant Felicity and others in her small band of believers. At this time in the Roman Empire, baptism and sharing the faith were capital crimes.

Perpetua's diary may be the oldest writing by a woman that we still have. In the appendix, written by a friend at her request, we find the description of her brutal death. In the arena, she was attacked by a wild heifer that wounded her but did not kill her. She passed out. When she regained consciousness, she asked that she be given pins to straighten her hair. In her day, a woman let her hair down in public only as a sign of mourning. She did not want spectators to think that she was grieving or afraid. Rather, even as she had to guide the inexperienced gladiator's hand for her own execution, she talked about the most exquisite joy of that moment. She rejoiced in her faith. She trusted that this ordeal would somehow be a ladder that took her into Jesus' arms.

Observers were shaken by both her treatment and her joy. How could she be joyful in the midst of horrible pain and death, leaving behind her small child and loving family? There can be only one source. That kind of unshakable joy, of spiritual bliss, is ours when we know that nothing can separate us from Christ. Not life. And not death. Joy in those circumstances wells up from the assurance that the Spirit meets our every need, and no matter where we are in life, the best is always yet to come.

Joy is not just a feeling. It is also a fierce power. It is a conduit of Spirit energy. In Scripture, joy is experienced in some of the most dire circumstances imaginable. In Paul's letter to his friends in Philippi, he rejoices at the beauty of faith itself and his friends' faithfulness. He rejoices in what is deeply true and unshakable, even while he is in a horrible prison with his feet chained into grooves in the wall and he sits in his own excrement. In that circumstance he tells his friends that they are his joy. He urges them, "Rejoice in the Lord always; again I will say, Rejoice" (Phil. 4:4). Why? Because joy is not rooted in what is happening around us or to us. It is rooted in what is happening eternally in Christ. For Christians, every day is seen in the context of eternity. Because joy is rooted in eternity, even suffering provides an opportunity for joy. It allows us to share in Jesus' own experiences of suffering and thereby to understand him and be closer to him.

During the contra war in Central America in the 1980s, I had the opportunity to travel with a small group of pastors and church educators to experience what was happening there. The hope was that we could see for ourselves and then be effective advocates and theological interpreters at home in the midst of complex and controversial policies. Our group stayed at a small retreat center in Costa Rica for the two weeks of our learning seminar.

One of our speakers was a woman from El Salvador who had escaped her country with the help of mission partners. Her husband had been a union organizer, which made them targets of the death squads. She told us about the night the soldiers stormed her home. She, her husband, and children had finished the evening meal and were in the kitchen washing up when the front door was forced open. The soldiers took her husband. They raped her and her young daughter and hung them in trees. They killed her son in her sight. Her daughter died beside her in the night.

In the morning, neighbors came to take down the bodies and found that the mother was still alive. They took her to mission workers who hid her, nursed her body, and made preparations to get her out of the country. Gradually, her body healed, but she refused to leave her town until she knew the fate of her husband. The day after she finally returned to her home, she was awakened at dawn by a knock on the door. She went to the door and found a small box containing a piece of her husband. This went on for several weeks. She did not leave until the daily boxes stopped coming and she had buried each one.

When she told us this story, I was shocked senseless. I had no idea what to do with that kind of brutality. The thing that was most confounding to me was her effervescent joy. Every part of her sparkled and twinkled. She made lovely artwork on beans that she sold to make a living. She was middle-aged but had luminous, unlined skin that glowed from within. One day at lunch I asked her how she had been able to endure what happened and how she had found such joy.

She told me that at first she thought she could not bear it. She wanted to die and prayed for death. The first few days that the dawn knocks came, she said that she literally threw up. But after a few days, she felt that the Spirit woke her up before the knock. She stood waiting for the package, breathing deeply and praying. As she went to the door each morning, she walked with the formal, deliberate steps of a bride. "All the way to the door," she said. "I just prayed the same prayer over and over. 'Thank you, Lord Jesus, for sharing your cross with me.'" I was speechless. She said, "Señorita, the joy of the Lord is my strength." The words in Nehemiah 8:10 had taken root in her and ripened.

Spirit joy flows from God's grace. It gives us power to go beneath our circumstances and find the deeper roots that cannot be moved or removed. Joy does not erase circumstances nor make them more palatable. It is not a Pollyanna optimism. Joy does not ripen when we repress, deny, or rewrite reality to make things seem better or more in line with our desires. Joy, rather, allows us to face life square on even when it is hard. Joy arises and helps us to awaken to the gift that life itself is, in all its ragged complexity.

Here is what I have learned, not least from the woman in Costa Rica: Spirit joy ripens in us when we realize that what we are experiencing has within it seeds for growth, unexpected grace, new insight and meaning. The Spirit gives us glimpses into what really matters in our situations and how each moment is a meaningful part of the whole fabric of our life. Joy grows and ripens as we move through the challenges of life.

JOY AND LAUGHTER

The Scripture, and life itself, teach us that joy is possible in every circumstance and that it is experienced in many different ways. Sometimes we experience joy as mirth. It is hard to not feel some measure of joy when spontaneous laughter erupts and lightens the heart.

Once when I had recently arrived at a new parish, I was busy in the sanctuary preparing for worship one Sunday morning. A young girl of about six came up to me to introduce a friend she had brought to worship. They were accompanied by her mom, who introduced me as Eugenia. After a hug, the little girl turned to her friend and said, "This is our new Genia. Our old Genia left, and we had to get a new one." Needless to say, joy bubbled up as laughter, and the whole worship service was infused with that special kind of lightness and wonderment.

Joy that issues in laughter is not just fun, it is healing. There is even a Laughter Online University (www .laughteronlineuniversity.com) that offers Laughter Wellness training for the purpose of creating a happier, healthier planet. Based on scientific evidence, they teach that laughter strengthens immune function and natural defenses to illness and claim that medical doctors all over the world prescribelaughter every day to their patients. The organization's website is filled with quotations from ancient times to modern about the benefits of laughter, including these: "As soap is to the body, so laughter is to the soul" (Jewish proverb). "Even the gods love jokes" (Plato). "At the height of laughter, the universe is flung into a kaleidoscope of new possibilities" (Jean Houston).[3]

I learned the value of laughter as a young child. I grew up in the storytelling culture of the Deep South, in which wild tales of humor and wit were the currency around our table at family celebrations. I was also a very sick child and spent many days home in bed or in hospitals under old-fashioned oxygen tents. Even in a wavy oxygen tent, I knew that laughing at Lucy and Ethel in the chocolate factory or stomping grapes was good medicine. *I Love Lucy* was the chicken soup of my early life. And I believe it helped. It is not possible to feel despair while laughing. Nor is it possible to give up.

Laughter connects. Even if we are alone when something strikes our funny bone, it still has a stimulus outside of ourselves. Maybe it is a meme someone posts online or a frolicsome bird we notice in the yard or a pet chasing rabbits in her sleep. Joy is always bigger than a solo experience, and it can bridge chasms in relationships that logic and debate only deepen.

In one of my favorite movies, *Moonstruck*, the family has gathered around the dining table. It is silent and tense. Big things are coming, and no one knows how it will all resolve. The old grandfather shatters the tension by saying, "Somebody tell a joke." It doesn't immediately change the situation or foretell the outcome, but it does lessen the tension and invisibly strengthen the family for what comes next. However we experience joy, even if it is a small smile in an MRI tube or a joke at the table of tension, there is always a partner in it. The Spirit is both its source and its unseen partner.

Be aware, though, that humor and joy are not always the same thing. Spirit joy is always positive. It never comes at someone else's expense. Humor can sometimes be pointed and mean-spirited, designed to denigrate someone behind the thin veil of "I was only joking." Just this week I saw a young man on television defend the most horrendous racist, misogynistic, anti-Semitic statements by claiming they were just jokes. Even though his words, spoken to an audience of like-minded people, elicited hoots of laughter and happiness, there was no Spirit joy there. Joy has no meanness. It is never barbed or backhanded. True joy that flows from the Spirit must be nurtured and tended with love.

RIPENING JOY

Even with all the Spirit joy moments that fill our lives, some of us Christians have cultivated joylessness as a kind of virtue. And it is not just us "dour Presbyterians" who sit up nights concerned that someone somewhere might be having a good time! As far back as the esteemed mystic John of the Cross in the sixteenth century, believers have contended that true virtue lay in tears over sin, more than in the spontaneous joy of salvation. Movies such as *Babette's Feast* and *Chocolat* depict the faithful as humorless self-deniers who need a dose of pagan feasting to remind them that they really are, as Paul puts it, "fools for Christ."

Sometimes Christians can behave as if we have missed the point altogether. We can come to think that Jesus' criticism of unfettered wealth and the hypocrisy of the elite, telling them they are laughing now but "will mourn and weep" (Luke 6:25), is an injunction against joy and laughter, not the blindness of self-righteousness and oppression. That beatitude, along with passages about picking up our crosses and the healing that comes through pain, can leave us thinking we must dutifully soldier on through this veil of tears trying to please a stern God and hoping that things will be better in heaven. We seem to think that is a feature of our seriousness of intent. Not so. Joy is the currency of heaven, to be sure, but it is also to be a mark of the here and the now, a fruit of the Spirit's presence in our everyday lives that can and should be nurtured and grown.

Joy is a muscle. We each must find the ways that are most natural for us to strengthen it. For some of us, worship ripens joy in us. The weekly rituals and disciplines, the relationships over time, the delights of music, word, and sacrament, strengthen joy in us as they deepen our spiritual lives. For many of us, nature ripens joy. Poet Elizabeth Barrett Browning wrote, "Earth's crammed with heaven, and every common bush afire with God."[4] John Calvin, so in love with the "theater of the creatures," urged his parishioners in Geneva not to cut down trees and to study bees to learn of God's ways. In that sense, all work for environmental justice is an act of praise that brings seeds of joy to fruit.

So many things can ripen joy if we permit it. Sometimes looking at a family album can strengthen joy. Or going for a walk. Or holding a sleeping child or pet. Beautiful art and music that touch us deeply strengthen our joy muscles. For some, physical exercise releases joy. Baking a cake or simply standing with a family member to wash the dishes after dinner awaken us to joy and allow it to strengthen within us and between us. It is our job to open our eyes and to linger there. Neuroscientists tell us that it takes at least fifteen seconds for joy to imprint on our neurons. Joy is for lingering over.

Joy is built up over a lifetime. In the summer of 2008, a month before my father died, he and my mother celebrated their sixtieth wedding anniversary. He was nearly bedridden by then from Parkinson's disease. All of their married life, my mother made his favorite dish for their anniversary. It was a complicated dish that nobody else in the family liked. That evening, once again they had shared that feast together. After supper, she helped ready him for the night and then went back out to the kitchen to clean up. When she got back to their room and got into bed next to him, she kissed him on the forehead and said, "Happy anniversary, darling." He took her hand in his trembling one and replied, "Hasn't it been grand?"

Those days were less than grand for them. And, as in any life, there were many that could not be so described. But still, what he recognized in that moment was the grandness of life shared. He felt the joy of loving and being loved. He felt the sweetness of heaven in a small smile. Joy ripens over time, as all life does, and it becomes sweeter and easier to find. Over years of ordinary life and growth, we can each find within us an unconquerable gladness that is rooted in the present moment and that bursts forth in moments as joy.

Even as joy ripens throughout a lifetime, there remains a childlike wonder about it. It thrives on the gentle trust of a child sleeping in a parent's arms. Trust in God's goodness, and our ultimate safety works quietly within our hearts to nurture joy. As a child I remember playing in our backyard under the old oak tree. I had a little tea set that had been passed down to me from my mother's childhood. I set it out in the afternoons, made moss sandwiches, and served tea in acorn hats to the fairies that lived in the gladioli condos in the flower garden. I felt utterly safe, and the world was full of wonders. Joy that is rooted in a sense of safety and wonder opens us, even as adults, to seeing wonders around us that the fears and the business of life shield from our eyes.

WEEDING AND TENDING
THE SPIRIT'S GARDEN OF JOY

Granted, there are many joy-stealers in each of our lives, congregations, and communities. Like a raccoon that gets to a ripening tomato just before it is ready to pick, feelings associated with painful memories, shame, fear, poor self-esteem, disappointment, resentment, remorse, recrimination, all can attack joy with sharp teeth. Those feelings lead to expectations that we will either be hurt again, or fail again, or be found out for the parts of ourselves that do not fit with our idealized picture of how life should be. Those moments of negativity and pain can rob us of the experience of joy. Many of us have spent far too much time ruminating over our fears and disappointments. We have built up a deep well of energy and pain inside us, one we are more accustomed to than we are to joy. For joy to ripen and become a way of life, we need to spend more time looking for it and experiencing it than we do dampening it.

The key to tending Spirit's joy is twofold. First, we need to decide that we will not resist our negative feelings. That seems counterintuitive, but resistance makes painful feelings only stronger. Rather than resist, we should simply allow them to be what they are, without giving them validation or attaching judgment. They are feelings we have developed over a lifetime in order to help us survive somehow. We do not need to control them or resist them. All we need to do is notice and release them to God.

When we do that, then negative energy begins to dissipate and we notice a new lightness. In that moment of lightness, we can decide to turn our hearts toward joy. Tending joy is about surrender more than mastery. To surrender the power of painful feelings over our lives and well-being, it helps to remember that what we focus on, we give power. It becomes our treasure (Matt. 6:19–21). It becomes our belief system. And what we believe, we enact.

When we are brave and willing to do the work of tending joy, the Spirit asks us, how long do you want to go on suffering? It is up to us. We can gently release the hurts and resentments that are joy-robbers, or we can cling to them. When we faithfully practice releasing negative emotions, we automatically stop resisting the positive ones.

Second, the simplest way to tend joy is to make the choice to consciously speak the words "thank you" throughout the day. When you do this slowly and with complete focus, you will begin to feel a depth of joy that is inside you and cannot be damaged by your fears or losses. Linger there. Give time to gratitude and to the things that make you smile. Remember that while joy is the Spirit at work in you, you are in charge of how and when you will experience it. You are also in charge of how and when you experience internal misery. Suffering is often out of our hands. We cannot always control what happens to us or the pain inflicted on us by others. Spirit joy, when sought and nurtured, even in times of hardship, is a grace through which we begin to see that though situations are miserable, there is more to us and every moment than our misery. This is not a smiley-faced denial of our circumstances. Rather it is a choice to look beneath those circumstances for Spirit joy that is more solid than any experience. "Thank you" is a powerful tool toward that end.

To tend Spirit joy, it is helpful to train ourselves to see the face of God everywhere. When you rise each morning, pray the simple prayer, "O God, show me your face today." When you see other people, notice them and thank God, saying something like, "O God, you are so beautiful." When you glance out the window or go for a walk or for a drink of water at work, notice the trees, the colors, the purity of the water, and pray, "O God, you are so beautifully displayed." Try to enter into the practice with a bright childlike trust and see what God surrounds you with every day. When this practice becomes a lifelong habit, joy will ripen in you and you will find it easier to access than you thought.

Too much change, uncertainty, and general cultural anxiety can be a weed in the garden of joy on a daily basis for any of us. When I was a pastor in Colorado, our church had a ministry with Hmong refugees from Southeast Asia. We sponsored families, helped to build small houses for them, and helped them learn English and secure work. That was the easy part.

We, and the community at large, were not so great at helping our new neighbors adapt to a dramatically different environment and culture. Before many months passed, a strange and terrible phenomenon arose. Young, apparently healthy men were dying in large numbers in their sleep. Doctors had no idea why this was happening.

When a reporter from the Denver newspaper interviewed the wives of these young men, they were not confused at all. They said they knew exactly what had caused the deaths of their husbands: evil spirits, processed food, and thinking too much.

We might not want to base a medical treatment plan on that theory, but I believe that most of us know how damaging thinking too much about either the past or our current troubles can be to our health and joy. If you notice yourself ruminating about anything in an unproductive way and begin to feel the energy drain from you and joy begin to evaporate, stop instantly, take several deep Spirit breaths, and allow what you are thinking about to take a shape in your mind's eye. Perhaps you will want to form it into a small ball of energy. Take the ball and toss it into the waiting hands of Jesus. As you toss it away, pray, "Take this burden from me, Lord. It is too heavy for me to carry. Fill its place in my heart with your presence and your joy. Thank you. Amen." Even if you pick up the ball again almost immediately, space will be clearing and joy will ripen.

CONCLUSION

The great sculptor Michelangelo, when asked how he got the inspiration to create a beautiful angel, responded, "I saw the angel in the marble and carved until I set him free."[5] Joy itself in these days is an act of resistance to the dominant pessimism, violence, and meanness that color too much of life. Our job as tenders of joy is to make space for it, to cut away the things that are not joy until the angelic is revealed. I invite you to chip away and see what is beautiful and joyful in your life that the Spirit wants to reveal.

A WEEK FOR TENDING JOY

Day One: "Weeping may linger for the night, but joy comes with the morning" (Ps. 30:5b). God's intention for each of our lives is that we live each day filled to the brim with joy and wonder. That doesn't mean that we never experience pain or challenges, but we know that they will not last forever and so we see them in a broader context. Ponder today some of the times when joy has broken through in your life even in the midst of hardship. What are the things that bring you joy? How can you incorporate those things into your life today? Thank God often today for the joy of God's presence that transforms any hardship.

Day Two: "His master said to him, 'Well done, good and trustworthy slave; you have been trustworthy in a few things; I will put you in charge of many things; enter into the joy of your master'" (Matt. 25:21). In this startling parable, Jesus shows us that what we do matters to God, and what we do for God matters supremely. The more we deepen in faith and service, the greater the joy we experience in our lives. What might you choose to do today that would allow God to say "Well done!" to you? How do you feel God's pleasure in your life? In what ways do you experience the joy of the Spirit? Thank God today for the joy of service, and ask how you might spread joy in all your actions and relationships.

Day Three: "I have said these things to you so that my joy may be in you and that your joy may be complete" (John 15:11). Jesus has just told his friends more about his relationship with the Father and the depth of the disciples' connection to him. Using the imagery of the vine and branches, he talks about abiding in us. Then he says an even more startling thing: *all* that he says to us is so that we can experience joy! Can you think of a time this week when joy erupted in laughter? God laughed with you. Can you think of a moment when you felt a centered small happiness? God shared that moment with you. What do you need today to make your joy complete? Ask God to speak to your heart on these matters and to fill you with the joy you are created to live.

Day Four: "Then he said to them, 'Go your way, eat the fat and drink sweet wine and send portions of them to those for whom nothing is prepared, for this day is holy to our LORD, and do not be grieved, for the joy of the LORD is your strength'" (Neh. 8:10). Ezra and Nehemiah have gathered the people of Israel together to encourage them and remind them of what is really important. They have returned to their war-ravaged land, and in their hearts, they believe the calamity was due to their own faithlessness. So the scribe and the governor get out the beautiful book of the Law and remind them of God's values and love. They tell the people that even though times are hard, they need not mourn, because God's own joy will lift their hearts and enable them to face whatever comes. Can you think of a time when God's joy bubbled up in you in a difficult time and made you strong? How do you access God's joy in your life? What are the most appropriate ways to share joy with others when they are facing difficulty? Ask God for guidance today. Ask God to deepen your joy and show you how it makes you strong.

Day Five: Read Ecclesiastes 3:1–8, which advises that there is "a time to weep and a time to laugh" (v. 4a). In this well-loved passage, the Wisdom writer gives us a picture of the fullness of life and basically says that everything in life fits. It all has a place, and it can all be used by God for healing and wholeness. Can you think of a time when weeping and laughing occurred together? What was the circumstance? How did the laughing impact the weeping?

Did you find that joy could be real for you in the midst of grief? Take a moment today to thank God for the healing power of joy.

Day Six: Read Acts 2:43–47, in particular verses 46–47a: "Day by day, as they spent much time together in the temple, they broke bread at home and ate their food with glad and generous hearts, praising God and having the goodwill of all the people." While the Greek word for joy is not used in this verse, Spirit joy suffuses the entire passage. Believers enjoyed God and enjoyed each other. It showed. Today, some Christians' lives and congregations seem to be marked more by fear, judgment, or apathy than simplicity, pure hearts, and joy. What are the most joy-filled aspects of your Christian community? How can you nourish contagious joy in your church? Take a moment today to thank God for other believers who join you on your journey. Pray that each one will experience Spirit joy today. As you talk to friends and family members, ask them to share the most joy-filled moment of their day. Thank God together for those moments.

Questions for Reflection and Discussion

1. In what ways do you regularly experience Spirit joy? How would you describe the difference between joy and happiness?

2. The German word *schadenfreude* describes a feeling of happiness because someone else struggles. Have you ever felt this kind of false joy? What are the circumstances in which you are prone to this, if you are? What would it take to replace this false joy with Spirit joy?

3. Joy is participatory. It is also more difficult for some of us than others. Neurologists tell us that an average six-year-old laughs six hundred times a day. Adults laugh fifteen to one hundred times a day. How can you nourish childlike laughter and wonder in your life and in your group?
4. What are the most effective joy dampeners in your life? How can you release them so that joy can bubble up more easily?
5. In what ways can you encourage the whole range of joy in your family, congregation, or community?

CHAPTER 4

TENDING THE
SHOOTS OF PEACE

All we are saying is give peace a chance.
—John Lennon

A former colleague of mine was vacationing with his family on the Mississippi Gulf coast. It was a beautiful day, and the whole family was excited about being at the shore. The only dampers on their enthusiasm were the double red flags indicating dangerous rip currents. My friend and his family had spent enough time on the coast to know that those flags had to be taken seriously, so they set up their umbrellas, unfolded their towels, handed out the bucket and spades, and prepared for a day of sand castles and slightly sandy drinks and sandwiches.

Very quickly they noticed another family nearby with five or six children. Apparently they did not see, or did not know to heed, the red flags. The whole family took off into the surf. It did not take long for the parents to realize the situation and begin to get all the children back to shore. They were able to round up all of them except for one little girl who was caught in the current.

Mercifully, a strong and experienced lifeguard was on duty. In a flash, he and his bodyboard were on their way to the child. When he reached her, she seemed more angry than scared. She had balled up her little fists and was pounding the water. As he approached, she pounded those fists at him too. Finally, when exhaustion nearly overcame her and she began to sink, he swooped in, got her on the board, and swam with her parallel to the beach until they escaped the current.

By the time he got her on shore, they were some distance down the beach. The little girl's family and a large crowd were worriedly pacing the shore when the lifeguard deposited the crying girl in her mother's arms. The father pumped the guard's hand in gratitude, asking, "Why did it take you so long to save her?" The guard responded, "Sir, I was with her the whole time, but I couldn't help her until she stopped fighting me."

My friend tells this story to make the point that God is with us at all times even if we are unaware or resistant. We can certainly say the same thing about all aspects of the fruit of the Spirit, perhaps none more than Spirit peace. It is often said that if you want peace, then stop fighting. That is certainly true. Still, is it really that simple? Sometimes yes. Sometimes no.

We call many things peace that are little more than a patch on a blown tire. The patch may help us survive if we blow a tire in the desert, but it will not make us more permanently secure. Only Spirit peace, released through us to a broken and fearful world, can do that heavy lifting.

Spirit peace is what happens when the world's indifference finally clears and is replaced by an all-encompassing compassion. This compassion at the heart of peace erases all boundaries and labels that permit division or the calcified understanding of anyone as enemy. We may certainly have opponents in life, those who thwart us, even harm us, but

Jesus made clear that enemies are to be a focus of our love and devotion to such an extent that the distinction disappears, as it did for the Good Samaritan (Luke 10:25–37).

We are not required to like, feel warm toward, or agree with opponents. We are required to love them, to see them as valuable, to see ourselves in them, and to see God's face mirrored in theirs, even if the faces are distorted and we can see only through a glass dimly.

Spirit peace is not achieved by repressing feeling or even actions of violence or negativity. Nor is it a product of mere self-control, as we will see in chapter 10. Peace is a totally Spirit-produced state of being in which our eyes clear and we begin to understand our responsibility for all others and for the earth itself.

Peace is not détente. It is not a grudging treaty that is breached in the heart before the ink dries. It comes from a recognition that we are all made of the same stardust. Peace emerges from knowing that we cannot fall out of God's arms, no matter how hard we wiggle, no matter how hard our little fists beat away the help that is always near.

PEACE IN THE NEW TESTAMENT

The biblical meaning of "peace" is much more nuanced than how we typically use the word in English. The word that Paul uses in his list of the fruit of the Spirit is *eirene*. It occurs in every book in the New Testament except 1 John. It refers to harmonious relationships between peoples, between nations, between a person and God, and within all the various aspects of a person that tend to war with each other. It has the connotation of quietness, freedom from oppression, rest, and contentment. It is the word used to describe internal coherence where all the pieces of our lives are knit together to fit into a new whole.

Eirene is the Greek word used to translate the Hebrew word *shalom*, which means wholeness, made perfect, or restored completely in every level of one's being. *Eirene*, like *shalom*, is the quality of living fully as God intended with nothing broken, nothing missing, nothing unfulfilled. These two words, *eirene* and *shalom*, remind us that God offers to give us well-being, assurance, and refuge.

Eirene is not the word that would be used for a truce when true reconciliation has not taken place or where resentments still fester and harmony exists only on the surface or is enforced. The peace that the Spirit ripens in us is not the absence of conflict per se. It is a quality of the inner and outer life that results both in and from the eradication of all hostility, envy, disquiet, and judgment.

Spirit peace is entirely different from the absence of conflict for which we often settle in our lives and in the world. It is a state of utter calm, contentment, harmony, health, wholeness, and acceptance. Spirit peace is utterly without need in the present moment and completely unfazed by the behavior of others. No wonder Jesus says in John 14:27, "Peace I leave with you; my peace I give to you. I do not give to you as the world gives. Do not let your hearts be troubled, and do not let them be afraid."

Peace is a part of the hope of Messiah. After the birth of John the Baptist, John's father, Zechariah, is moved by the Spirit to prophesy. His beautiful poem of prophecy in Luke 1:67–79 ends with this heartfelt longing: "Because of the tender mercy of our God, the dawn from on high will break upon us, to shine upon those who sit in darkness and in the shadow of death, to guide our feet into the way of peace." Here Zechariah stands in the centuries-old tradition of Isaiah, who said, "For a child has been born for us, a son given to us; authority rests upon his shoulders, and he is named Wonderful Counselor, Mighty God, Everlasting

Father, Prince of Peace. Great will be his authority, and there shall be endless peace for the throne of David and his kingdom" (Isa. 9:6–7a). This has always been at the heart of Israel's messianic hope, even when life and faithlessness sometimes obscured the reality of that hope and left the people crying with Jeremiah, "'Peace, peace,' when there is no peace" (Jer. 8:11).

By the time of Jesus, the word *eirene* was a common greeting, just as *shalom* became in Hebrew. It was a way of wishing another well, hoping that there will be no damaging conflict in their lives. When we hear it from Jesus' lips, it takes on deeper and more personal connotation.

Days after Jesus' brutal death, his closest friends are still reeling, wondering what can happen next, when Mary Magdalene bursts in, telling them that Jesus is no longer in the tomb. The men go and look. True, he is not there, but he does not meet them in the garden or on the road. Mary Magdalene says that he has risen from the dead and that she talked to him in the garden outside the tomb. The men don't know what to think. They believe that they are in danger no matter what has happened. In John 20:19, Jesus' friends are huddled behind locked doors, trembling with fear and confusion. Then Jesus walks right through their locked doors, says, "Peace be with you," and gives them their mission. He tells them to do in his name what he did in the Father's. They are undone.

Thomas isn't with them, however, and when they tell him later what has happened, he makes it clear that he could have been born in Missouri, the Show Me State. He wants to see in order to believe. He has been called the Doubter for millennia, and yet the word for doubt does not appear in the Greek text. When Jesus arrives to meet his need, to give him the same experience that the others had, he simply encourages him not to be distrustful, but to trust his own experience.

When Jesus greets Thomas with the word "peace," he offers him his own intimate presence. He offers Thomas the opportunity to enter into Jesus' wounds as a way of coming to trust and experience peace. The peace that Jesus offers to Thomas, and to all of us, often comes most directly in times when trust is lagging. We, like Thomas, experience it by entering into the wounds of Jesus, stretching our hand into his side, right into his heart. In other words, it is intimacy with the whole of Jesus' life and love that allows us to live with and from peace. It allows us to remember what is real and true in our lives. After all, one of the hallmarks of war and division is forgetting who we are and whose we are. Spirit peace allows us, as the body of Christ, to offer our own wounds to a brokenhearted world. Jesus, in offering his wounds to Thomas, invites us to ponder that the way to peace can sometimes come through hurt and rejection. Sometimes we, too, will get bloodied by love and come out the other side to experience Spirit peace.

From the church's earliest days, we have found it hard to live in peace and to offer *shalom* to those in our churches or to the world. In Corinth, the congregants fought about everything. They fought about what was appropriate in worship and who was allowed to speak for the sake of order. They fought about how to raise money. They fought about sex. They fought about power. They were a laughingstock in the community because they got so upset in worship that they sometimes dragged each other out by the hair and sued each other in civil court.

What Paul recognized in these conflicts was the power of divisions to lead to spiritual amnesia. Lack of peace results from a series of false steps away from being our true selves, whether that is people pleasing, expediency, despair, fatigue, the love of money and power, or shutting down our own feelings in order to be more acceptable to others. It all leads to the same disquiet and dissatisfaction that inevitably lead to divisions and conflict.

OBSTACLES TO SPIRIT PEACE

Peace can be nearly impossible to access in times of hardship or grief. Still, not being fully at peace can be a grace sign pointing us to look more deeply to the Spirit, who is always at peace. Spirit peace does not require us to accept the unacceptable. If we are hungry, oppressed, mourning, or frightened, it is hard to even remember what peace can feel like. Even so, the Spirit remains within us in our difficult circumstances, nudging us, if only for a moment, to observe the situation with Spirit-empowered eyes. When we are able to do that, even briefly, pathways to action often occur to us. Having a plan and seeing the next step helps restore the flow of Spirit peace.

If we are not in danger and still find peace lacking, then something is blocking that flow. What exactly that blockage is will be different for each of us. In the Thomas story, we see that peace can be hampered by lack of trust. Through the early church's conflicts, we see that peace is difficult in a context of power skirmishes and the need to control others. Whatever we determine our block to be, it will likely contain faulty memory, faulty expectations, faulty self-perception, faulty theology, or trying to please or control people.

Shortly after I moved to Colorado, on a beautiful Saturday afternoon when the sky was clear and blue, the air was crisp with the coming winter, and the aspen trees were shimmering gold in the mountain winds, a group of new friends took me for an afternoon of exploring in the high country. We traveled on the interstate west of Denver, past the little mining towns of Idaho Springs and Silver Plume, past the ski resorts of Loveland, Copper Mountain, and Vail. Then we turned off on a ragged state road with hairpin turns that wound through tiny towns tucked in cliffs, beside incredible ravines. It was beautiful, exciting, and disorienting to my southern self.

As we drove, we made an impossible sharp curve and spotted a little white town perched on a cliff overlooking a deep valley and surrounded by fourteen-thousand-foot peaks. There appeared to be one road that led into and out of the town. The road was barricaded closed with one of the iron swing-arm gates that I would soon learn swung in front of entrance ramps and at crossroads to close roads due to snow. Attached to the gate was a stark white sign, "Town for Sale." We pulled up in front. "It's a ghost town," my new friends said.

We got out and climbed over the barricade and began to explore. It was a beautiful little town with white frame houses, simple and neat. Some had Victorian touches like gingerbread on the porches or even a little widow's walk. Some were a little larger, some a little smaller. There was a tiny red post office, a little one-room school with a play yard and seesaws at odd angles. There was a front street with a general store, a café, a sewing store, and a toy store. There was a vacant lot with a sign flapping and clanking on an old chain for snowmobiles and snowblowers. There was a little white frame church with a bell still visible in the tower.

As we wandered the streets, I was amazed at how neat the abandoned town still was. There were a few windows out, but most still had colored ruffled curtains hanging in them. A few porches had window boxes that had fallen. Some even had pansies growing up through the broken wood of the boxes. Few houses had lawns, so there was no telltale uncut grass to give the town away. There were aspen trees, glimmering and shimmering in the sunshine. It simply looked like everyone had stepped out for lunch.

"What happened?" I asked.

"This was a company town for one of the mines that shut down a year or so ago. No mine. No town." We walked on in silence for a few moments, past a house with a handmade cradle on the front porch, past a rock garden still in bloom, past abandoned woodpiles and a broken tricycle. I began to cry.

"What's wrong with you?" my friends asked. "I don't know," I said. "I just want to leave." They shrugged, and we got back in the car. I was still crying. "It's just so sad. All the dreams. All the life. All the promise is gone. All that's left is the window dressing."

Later that night, I wondered why the town had had that effect on me. I realized that I, too, was a bit of a ghost town. Full of dreams, life, and promise, if not gone, at least at risk.

I was far away from home. My ministry was in transition. My personal life was in shambles I would not admit to myself, and I spent an enormous amount of energy hiding all of that from everyone else. Like a picket-fenced mountain town that looked good on the outside but held nothing of life within, like a whitewashed tomb that looked good but came with a warning not to touch, I was in trouble. I was a roiling mess of inner conflicts, and I did not know what to do.

What I have learned since that painful moment of self-awareness is that peace cannot share space with the false self that ego has developed to protect us from our own truth. Nor can peace share space in the heart with a kind of false nostalgia in which we cling to an idealized picture of how things were but never actually were. That only seduces us to believe that the state that never was can come again, and when it does, then everything will be right with the world.

When we give up our true selves and have no will but that which others, or our idealized version of things, have for us, there can be no peace. When we accept lies as truth and organize our lives around those lies, suppressing any truth that calls them into question, there can be no peace. When we find ourselves mere ghost towns, looking good on the outside but holding no internal coherence on the inside, we will be strangers to peace and will constantly look for someone or something outside ourselves to blame.

When we think that things must turn out a certain way for us to survive and be happy, peace will not flourish within us or flow easily from us. When we think, even subconsciously, that other people were put on this earth to do what we think they should do, to fill up holes in our hearts, or to accomplish what we cannot for ourselves, our relationships will not be marked by peace. It is hard to maintain Spirit peace when we think that our peace is in someone else's hand and that we are therefore helpless. As long as we make peace dependent on what someone else says, does, or chooses, we will not live in peace.

It is hard to grasp, but nonetheless true, that Spirit peace is always experienced unilaterally. Truces, treaties, the end of wars, those things are bilateral. Peace is unilateral. It is a decision made in the soul. It grows and matures within the self. It is a reality at the core of our being and can be called on, or awakened to, when we are our truest selves. Otherwise, peace will always be sullied with need and dependence on things that can never deliver.

We can often strangle out peace in Spirit's garden when we think that somehow God is not capable of, or interested in, managing the universe, because it doesn't seem to be managed in a way that makes sense to us. Frequently when that secret belief emerges it comes with an exaggerated sense of our own importance. We can come to think that we are responsible for everything. We, only we, can fix it, whatever it is. We can easily then lose all sense of peace and perspective, because we are not equipped to be responsible for everything. Often this tangle of emotions arises from some wound that we are desperately trying not to replicate.

For example, from the memory around my grandmother's death that I shared in chapter 1, I learned not only that God was ever present in times of trial but also that some things hindered my peace as well. As I was being led away from the family and friends gathered to support us in our loss, I was also physically moving away from my vivid experience of God's presence surrounding my grieving family. From that, a part of me learned to try to escape my painful emotions at all costs. I learned that others thought I was not strong enough to face my life and losses. And, as I learned many years later in studying childhood grief, I probably, as most children do, internalized the loss as my fault. I had not kept my grandmother alive as I was "expected" to do. Not only that, she had abandoned me. I must have done something terribly wrong. So I took on the utterly peace-robbing role of keeping churches, relationships, and even faulty dreams alive at all cost. Until I learned to see how I and others had added burdensome layers to what that small child internalized, I rarely had moments of real peace. I was too busy trying to be God without the necessary equipment.

PEACE AND THE ENEMY

When I met Archbishop Desmond Tutu during a small luncheon of church leaders when he visited Birmingham, Alabama, in 2002, he told me, "If you want peace, you don't talk with your friends. You talk with your enemies." Over the years as I have pondered the truth of that statement, I have come to believe that a part of the job of peacemaking rests on our willingness to be vulnerable in order to be real. It is only shared realness that can transform a heart and allow a person to lay down arms and erase the notion of enemy.

Spirit peace insists that we stop the cycles of violence that surround us on so many levels both outside of us and inside of us and decide that we, as Paul urges, will "not repay anyone evil for evil" (Rom. 12:17). To do that we must open ourselves to the deep truth that we are all children of the same Parent. We all have limitations, weaknesses, and ragged broken hearts that often cut others on their edges. To experience mature peace with those we call enemy, we come to realize that they are neither more flawed nor more special than anyone else, including ourselves.

When we see someone as an intractable enemy or antagonist, that is often a marker that we ourselves have inner work to do. To practice peace, to make room for it to emerge in our hearts, will reveal to us the indestructibility of our own being and of others. Laying down our arms, embracing as siblings those we do not agree with or find it difficult to tolerate, changes the lens through which we see the world, its problems, and our own.

Spirit peace is not a constant felt condition in this life, sadly. But when it dawns, it is like the blinds going up on a sparkling day to reveal the wild and perfect sea. Then we realize that all our prayers for peace are answered, even those we have not found words to pray, and Jesus' promise, "Peace I leave with you; my peace I give to you" (John 14:27), ripens and becomes an observable characteristic of our lives and ethics. We do not conjure up this peace, but we do have to claim it and put it into practice in our lives.

One sunny Tuesday morning, I got a phone call. It was one of "those" phone calls, in which a crying friend informed me of the death of another dear friend. Anthony and I had been friends since the seventh grade. He had a much more profound role in my life than I in his, without a doubt. When my friend told me what had happened, any feeling of peace I might have had evaporated. I was furious. We were supposed to have a shrimp dinner on my porch this summer. We had only recently been talking about our dreams for the last chapters of our lives. And now Anthony had died. I was undone. As my friend ended our conversation, he said, "Anthony, bro, rest in peace."

What do we really mean when we say that? Is it a prayer for the afterlife? A hope that the one who has died will not feel the utter lostness that we do in saying good-bye? Is it just something we grab hold of like a hand when we are slipping down a mountainside? Perhaps it is all of that. Still, as I heard my friend say those well-worn words, I felt something else at work as well. Perhaps that phrase is not so much our prayer as the Spirit's prayer within us in the presence of all pain and grief. "Rest in peace, my child. You will know more soon. But for now, rest in my peace that can even soften the mystery of death." Perhaps that is even what Jesus was saying to his friends on the night of his betrayal, "My peace I give to you" (v. 27), and on the day of his rising, "Why are you weeping? . . . Peace be with you" (20:13, 21).

WORKING IN THE GARDEN OF PEACE

Many of us did not have the resources to deal with our hurts in the moments when they occurred. Perhaps we were children or in danger or simply overwhelmed. When the wounds of the past are not properly dealt with, the emotions associated with those experiences can get sticky and attach to other events in the present moment. Even if we have mentally put to rest whatever happened to us, unless the emotions are processed and released, they can keep us spiraling in one turmoil after another. Have you ever had an emotional response to something and known that it was outsized? Have you ever felt that you were overreacting and not been sure why? If so, you may be dealing with sticky emotions that have been triggered and have nearly nothing to do with what is going on at the moment. Those emotions need tending for peace to ripen.

It is possible to release the hold of those emotions with the Spirit's help. It doesn't usually happen quickly, but with practice over time, awareness of what is happening in you will grow, and the emotions will have less power over your life and behavior. This will create a space where peace can emerge and flower.

To begin to work on this section of your soul garden, set aside some time to be alone, without external distractions. Some of what rises may be heavy. If it feels like too much, take small steps. You can do this important work when you are ready and at your own pace. If you find that the wound is deep and the trauma great, seek support before you begin.

Take several deep breaths and release each one slowly. Invite the Spirit to help you with this exercise. Ask the Spirit if there is an incident or a wound that you need to work with today. Give space for something to arise. Then, in a journal, write everything that you can think of about what happened. Be as honest as you possibly can. When you think you have finished, keep going for a moment more.

Then, still in the context of prayer, see if you can identify the emotions you felt in that situation. Remember that what you are considering is of the past. It is not happening to you now, and you can stop and return to your safe, quiet place anytime you choose. You might even want to practice shifting from the memory to the present moment a few times so that you know you are safe.

What did you learn about yourself and the world from what happened to you? Is any of that true? Are there times now when you act as if those things are true in the present moment when they are not? When you have had time to consider, offer the memory of what happened to God for healing. Ask the Spirit to shift the way you think about these things and to help you release the past to the past. Take with you only the learnings that are meaningful and true. Thank God for lightening your burden, and go into your day a little more at peace.

Perhaps painful memories do not threaten your peace. Still you may wonder, how do we nourish peace when wars rage all around us and within us? How do we nourish peace when we are confused and can't tell right from wrong, better from best? How do we nourish peace when our hearts are breaking about things over which we have no control? How do we lay down arms in our inner lives that are so often filled with harsh judgments, guilt, and shame? How do we lay down the burdens of fear and disappointment that keep us agitated and angry? How do we allow a swell of peace to emerge from the tear-soaked ground of our memories? Perhaps the best we can do is to pray regularly and with open hearts the prayer of Francis of Assisi and make room for the Spirit to do the winsome work only the Spirit can do.

Lord, make me an instrument of your peace.
Where there is hatred, let me sow love;
where there is injury, pardon;
where there is doubt, faith;
where there is despair, hope;
where there is darkness, light;
where there is sadness, joy.
O Divine Master, grant that I may not seek so much
to be consoled as to console,

to be understood as to understand,
to be loved as to love.
For it is in giving that we receive,
it is in pardoning that we are pardoned,
and it is in dying that we are born to eternal life. **Amen.**[6]

CONCLUSION

Spirit peace operates on many levels. We can experience it between individuals, groups, and peoples. It is available for us to release in every situation of tension or discomfort. The Spirit is content, and when we learn to harvest the Spirit's peace, we can access that contentment as a resource for ourselves. Peace is not about the end of conflict in and of itself. It is a unilateral choice we make based on compassion for our shared humanity. It results in wholeness and a broader view of every situation. It is the source of the cessation of conflict as well as the result. Spirit peace begins in hearts that bravely face the truth personally and in the world.

It is important to remember that Spirit peace requires, first of all, the willingness to come to know ourselves as we are so intricately and lovingly created. To mature in peace takes time, hope, courage, and a resolute determination to stop causing harm to others and ourselves. We can make that choice, empowered by the Spirit, even if others do not.

The Trappist monk Thomas Merton (1915–68) described the feeling of Spirit peace in a diary entry just six days before his death:

"I was suddenly, almost forcibly, jerked clean out of the habitual half-tied vision of things, and an inner clearness, clarity, as if exploding from the rocks themselves, became evident and obvious. . . . There is no puzzle, no problem, and really no 'mystery.' All problems are resolved and everything is clear, simply because what matters is clear."[7]

Awakening to the peace of God's love-saturated long view in which we come to know that all is well, and will be well, is Spirit peace fully ripened.

A WEEK FOR TENDING PEACE

Day One: "Blessed are the peacemakers, for they will be called children of God" (Matt. 5:9). In the Sermon on the Mount, Jesus sums up the whole of his teaching and values. The word translated as "blessed" in the Beatitudes means "happy" or "in a good condition." Jesus tells us that those who work for peace are not only happy and in a good place but also heirs of all that God has and have an honored share in God's household. How can you be a peacemaker today? Are there people in your life toward whom you have hard feelings or are carrying a grudge? Is there room for change there? Are there warring ideas or issues within your own heart? How might the blessedness of Christ's peace put that right? Ask God today to bring a new measure of peace into your heart, relationships, and priorities. Notice any feelings of peace and give thanks.

Day Two: "I have said this to you so that in me you may have peace. In the world you face persecution, but take courage: I have conquered the world!" (John 16:33). The world is not at peace. Even we ourselves are often not at peace. Yet it is clear that the state of harmony is Jesus' intention for us. Jesus tells us that the hope of peace rests in him. We can move into peace because he has dealt with all that tears us apart. In what way can Jesus enter into your heart today to bring you peace of mind? How do the small decisions you make each day affect the peace of the world? The peace of the good earth itself? How can you work for peace and harmony in the world? Choose one small thing that you can do as an act of faith. Thank God for the gift of peace and pledge yourself to live in peace each day.

Day Three: "May the God of hope fill you with all joy and peace in believing, so that you may abound in hope by the power of the Holy Spirit" (Rom. 15:13). Paul writes this benediction after quoting a lovely poem of praise to God. He is approaching the end of his life, although he probably does not know that. He has faced persecution, imprisonment, ridicule, rejection, and poverty. He has also known the bliss of Christ's presence and the joy of serving and sharing Christ with others. He tells us that the key to joy and peace is found in "believing," using a Greek word that means "trusting." Our trust in God is the source of much of our joy and all of our peace! Are there areas of your life in which you need to deepen your trust? Are there areas in which you resist trusting? What are the consequences of that resistance? Take time today to silently repeat the prayer, "I trust you, Lord." Do this especially with anything that is troubling you or over which you seem to have no control. Thank God for the new peace you are experiencing this week and commit to deepen your trust day by day.

Day Four: "Peace I leave with you; my peace I give to you. I do not give to you as the world gives. Do not let your hearts be troubled, and do not let them be afraid" (John 14:27). Jesus and his disciples are in the upper room together on the fateful night of his betrayal. They have shared the sacred Passover meal. He has washed their feet and given them the fresh commandment to love one another. Now he is preparing them for his departure. He has promised them the Holy Spirit as comforter, defender, and guide. All that is left is for him to wish them peace, wholeness, well-being, and all the courage that comes with those things. We need those things ourselves when we face difficult days and impossible situations. Take a moment to quiet your mind and slow your breathing. Ask God to awaken you to the Spirit's deep peace that resides within you. If you are experiencing fear or confusion, offer those things to God and ask for peace and insight. Notice what comes.

Day Five: "And the peace of God, which surpasses all understanding, will guard your hearts and your minds in Christ Jesus" (Phil. 4:7). God's peace, even when regularly released in us and put to work in our lives, remains a mystery. How can we experience deep peace in the midst of the worst possible circumstances, like those Paul faced in prison, where he wrote this letter? Sometimes we don't, but we know that we can. Paul reminds us that peace guards our hearts and minds. This means that God's complete well-being can order our thinking and our actions. Take time throughout the day to ask the Spirit's peace to emerge and order your thoughts and actions. Notice what happens.

Day Six: "For God is a God not of disorder but of peace" (1 Cor. 14:33). The Corinthian church is in turmoil. Paul is addressing the theological and spiritual conflict that has arisen around the gift of speaking in tongues. Those with the gift think that everyone should have it and that they are holier and closer to God because they do. Those with different gifts think that the tongues speakers are, if not crazy, then divisive and arrogant. In this verse, Paul reminds all of them that God is not the author of disorder, disputes, and divisions. God brings Spirit peace, unity, and reconciliation, not defiant lines drawn in the sand. Can you think of times when you, or others, have claimed God's sanction on judging or shaming others? Can you think of times in the life of the church when people divided up in sides, each claiming that God is on their side? Differences are not evil. We can grow from dialogue with those with whom we disagree. How do we learn to disagree in peace? What needs to change in order for that capacity to grow?

Questions for Reflection and Discussion

1. When you think of peace as the translation of *sha-lom,* wholeness, what are the qualities of wholeness in individual lives that you think the Spirit desires? What about in communities? Congregations? The global family?
2. Peace encompasses not just the human family and its institutions. It also includes peace for the whole created order. In what ways do you see the earth and its creatures longing for peace? What would "peace on earth" look like?
3. What are patterns of thought and feelings that must be touched for Spirit peace to come to maturity in your life? Family? Congregation?
4. Does conflict ever have a role in leading to peace? If so, how? How would you describe the difference between the absence of conflict and Spirit peace?
5. Can you think of a time when you seemed to be a stranger to peace? What led to this? How do you find your way through those times? Are there practices that help you that you can share with your group?

CHAPTER 5 *peace*

⟨co⟩⟨co⟩

TENDING THE
SHOOTS OF PATIENCE

Trees that are slow to grow bear the best fruit.
—Molière

When I was growing up, my friend Lucille was known for many things. She was a sweet, funny, madcap, tiny, loyal, cheerleadery kind of person. She and her sister Laura were twins in a family with two sets of twins. Lucille was perhaps most renowned for two facts: when she drove, you couldn't see her over the steering wheel, and she could not wait for Christmas Day to open her presents.

Starting in midsummer she began to save her allowance to stockpile wrapping paper, which she hid under her bed. When the Christmas season approached, she did weekly forensic searches of the house, the car, all of her mother's favorite hiding places. When she found a present for herself, she locked herself in the bathroom with identical wrapping paper, ribbon, scissors, and tape. She carefully unwrapped each present, inspected it, rewrapped it, and put it back in its hiding place. There were no surprises for Lucille on Christmas morning. I once asked if it made Christmas morning less special. She seemed bumfuzzled by the question. "Why would it?" she asked. "I still get all the stuff." I never really knew if Lucille was lacking in patience or just couldn't stand suspense. In either case, there was not a present with her name on it safe from the weekend of Thanksgiving onward.

Patient waiting for good things, or waiting out the bad things, is not a prominent mark of our culture in the United States. We expect a lot of instant. We want our food fast, our texts responded to with lightning speed, and our news a constant stream of sound bites. We want diet results fast, spiritual growth instantly, and health and vigor restored after a setback as if nothing ever happened. We time our waits in line and on tech support, and the length of those waits can determine our state of mind as we do what needs to be done. Patience is not our cultural strong suit.

The first three aspects of the fruit of the Spirit—love, joy, and peace—are like a waltz. One two three. One two three. When we have learned their dance, the other aspects join us on the dance floor. The first of the new partners is patience. It is even more confounding than the first three or learning to wait in line without erupting like a volcano.

The word that Paul chooses in Galatians 5:22 is not the more common word translated as patience in Scripture. That word, *hypomone*, refers to cheerful, hopeful endurance. It is a deeper form of patience than waiting out the calendar until Christmas. It has the sense of waiting with wonder for the Lord. This word recognizes that there is grace in everything if we will stop and look. It comes from knowing that good is always on the way, that God is never helpless, and that good will arrive for us soon. As daunting a quality as that is to cultivate these days, the word Paul chooses is more daunting still.

Paul chooses the Greek word *makrothymia*. It is sometimes translated "long-suffering" or "forbearance." It literally means "long temper." This word refers to that quality of self-restraint in the face of provocation or wrong that does not hastily retaliate or promptly punish, even when one could or it would seem justified to do so. It refers to a quiet, waiting wisdom and compassion that does not surrender to circumstances or succumb under trial. It is not passive. It is concentrated and controlled strength that is at the same time mild, compassionate, and constant in all circumstances. The opposite of *makrothymia* is quick anger, self-righteous retaliation, and a grumbling spirit. I like to define *makrothymia* as the quality of having a long and supernaturally compassionate fuse. It is not a natural human trait. It is a supernatural aspect of the Spirit's work in a person.

PATIENCE IN THE BIBLE

In the Hebrew Scriptures, patience is revealed as the characteristic of God that allows God to temper righteous anger. Psalm 86:15 gives us a beautiful picture of God's predominant temperament: "But you, O Lord, are a God merciful and gracious, slow to anger and abounding in steadfast love and faithfulness." Slowness to anger arises from the depths of God's love and faithfulness to God's people, even when we stray far from God's values. God continually reins in God's frustration at our self-defeating, other-harming behaviors and seeks ways for us to start again.

This quality of God's patience arises from God's steadfast love. In Micah 6:8, when the dire consequences of Israel's continued faithlessness can no longer be denied and the people go to God begging to be told what to do to regain the standing and protection of God that they feel they have lost due to their own sin, God gives them a simple formula for their behavior. It is also as good a description of who God is as can be found in the Scripture. "What does the LORD require of you but to do justice and to love kindness and to walk humbly with your God?"

The word we translate as "kindness" in this verse is *hesed*. It describes a reality that is deep and fundamental to God's nature and to life as God's people. In various passages in the Old Testament, the word is translated as loving-kindness, steadfast love, faithfulness, grace, mercy, or devotion. The concept is always relational and refers to the quality of relationships intended in covenant life. *Hesed* has within it a sense of obligation and generosity. In the vast majority of instances, the word refers to God's covenantal relationship with Israel. I like to translate it as "unshakeoffableness." It is God's loving-kindness that slows God's anger and keeps God coming back again and again to seek to restore relationship with Israel and to establish the beloved community of *shalom*.

God's steadfast love is bounteous, abounding, and plentiful. It never gives up. *Hesed* is the particular love that God has for God's people. God's love affirms that human beings will never be abandoned no matter what the circumstances, not even for breach of covenant. God will always find a way to love us into wholeness. This kind of love is not a natural attribute of human beings. As a matter of fact, the only human in the Bible who is described with that word is Ruth in her steadfast devotion to her bereft mother-in-law, Naomi. Still, the capacity is within us and necessary for patience to take root. Spirit patience can be experienced only when we have committed not to run away, seek the easiest path, or somehow get recompense from someone who has harmed us.

Testimony to the capacity of God to keep a long fuse (because of God's steadfast love) abounds in the Old Testament. The depiction of God in Exodus 34:6, "The

LORD, the LORD, a God merciful and gracious, slow to anger, and abounding in steadfast love and faithfulness," shows up in similar forms in Psalm 103:8; Jonah 4:2; Micah 7:18; and throughout the book of Hosea, where God's loving patience is a major theme.

For Christians, Jesus is our divine model of what long-suffering patience looks like in human life. As he approached Jerusalem for the final time, Jesus stopped and wept over the city. He had just soundly denounced the hypocrisy of the establishment leaders. He knew full well what that would mean for him and soon. He could have lost patience with the people and their recalcitrance. He could have called on armies of angels to wipe them out and start over. Yet what did he choose? He chose to weep for us instead of protecting himself. Like a mother who cannot understand why her child is set on self-destruction, Jesus pauses and says, "Jerusalem, Jerusalem, the city that kills the prophets and stones those who are sent to it! How often have I desired to gather your children together as a hen gathers her brood under her wings, and you were not willing! See, your house is left to you, desolate" (Matt. 23:37–38). That is a picture of long-suffering patience.

Later when Jesus is with his friends in the Garden of Gethsemane, he asks them to pray with him, but they cannot stay awake. He tries to wake them several times, until finally his patience takes over and he anguishes alone while allowing them to take rest in sleep. Only when the results of the betrayal begin to unfold and the crowd and temple police descend on him does he wake his disciples to face what is coming. Even then, he greets Judas as a friend. When the disciples realize what is happening, one of them takes to the sword and cuts off the ear of the slave of the high priest. "Then Jesus said to him, 'Put your sword back into its place, for all who take the sword will die by the sword" (Matt. 26:52). If there was ever a picture of a supernaturally long fuse, that is it. He does not lash out, although he certainly could have. He does not retaliate, although he certainly would have seemed warranted to do so. He shows compassion to those caught up in the betrayal, even the betrayer himself. There is warmhearted mercy even as he is startled and appalled by their actions.

Makrothymia recognizes that when we respond in kind, we set in motion dynamics in our hearts and relationships that cannot easily be turned around. Like the prophetic word once spoken, retaliation always goes its own way once released. There is no stopping it. When our impulse is to respond in anger or judgment but we refrain from doing so and reframe the situation with mercy and compassion, that is Spirit patience at work in us.

SPIRIT PATIENCE IN OUR LIVES

As someone who is currently learning to live with chronic pain, even the word "patience," or especially "long-suffering," often produces the opposite effect. I want to fight. In a way, that is not a bad thing. It produces enough energy in me to get me up off the couch most days. I find, though, that I am often like the young man who went to the wise spiritual director and asked the wise one to pray that he would develop patience. The old man stopped right then and prayed with the man, saying, "Dear Lord, give this young man tribulation in the morning. Give him tribulation at noonday. Give him . . ." The young man stopped him and said, "Wait! I asked you to pray for patience, not tribulation." The old wise one said, "Well, young man, tribulation is the only way you will ever get to patience."

I do not believe that God brings hardship on us to teach or to deepen us or for any other reason. I do know that learning lies in how we react to what happens to us, not in the hardship itself. As the apostle Paul learned in prison and with his own mysterious thorn in the flesh from which he prayed for relief his whole life, the powerful aspects of the Spirit are a part of us as the Spirit indwells us, even when we do not feel it or are disappointed that God is not a puppet on a string to instantly answer our prayers exactly as we desire.

Years ago I was traveling from a retreat center in Mississippi, where I had finished a teaching event, and was on my way to Memphis for another one. I stopped for lunch with a woman I had known for a number of years when we worked together on projects for Presbyterian Women. Margaret was one of the most beautiful women I have ever known. She was older than me by probably thirty years and yet she felt like a contemporary to me. For the last six months, Margaret had been enduring treatments for a fast-moving cancer. When I stopped that day, she had that telltale grayness to her skin tone but her smile and warmth were genuine, as they always were. We sat on a bench in her garden. It was fall, and the leaves were changing. There was the beginning of crispness to the air. She had made us iced tea and scones, warm with butter and cream. We talked about everything and nothing until finally I got up my courage to ask how the treatment was going. "Well," she said, "we will have to wait and see. But today is just lovely, isn't it?" Consummate professional that I am, I burst into tears. "Drink your tea, Eugenia," she said, her sweet spirit never wavering. "It is perfect."

It was not clear at the time if she was speaking of the tea or the day or our visit or her own trials. But suddenly in that moment I knew with certainty that she was right and all those things were included in God's perfect moment that we shared together.

Margaret had awakened to the utter amazement of life itself, lived in the presence of and for God. One of the gifts that Spirit patience gives, and relies on, is the capacity to allow things to be as they are without undue fight or protest. Beneath our circumstance lives something perfect. Spirit patience releases in us the wisdom to know how fruitless it is to rail against what we are experiencing. It offers us the capacity to allow the rain to enter into the heart without resorting to emotional flight or deflecting fight. Spirit patience renders "if only" moot. There was nothing needed in that perfect fall moment Margaret and I shared that was not already present. When we decide not to fight our experience, then suddenly it feels inexhaustibly holy and we can sink into the beauty of life even if we hurt or fear or grieve.

WEEDS IN PATIENCE'S GARDEN

The desire to avoid all pain can choke out Spirit patience. Humans will do almost anything to not feel pain, including causing others pain, defying healthy boundaries, and abusing power. At least some of the time, most of us can find a mental gymnastics routine to rationalize, justify, or blame someone else for our painful circumstances. These strategies never work for long and wind up drawing to us more calamity from which we want to go numb.

Sometimes in these circumstances, we run to the moral evils Paul lists in Galatians 5 and a whole host of others that we design for ourselves. We do these things not because we want to or because we enjoy "being bad." We do them because on some skewed level we believe that they will lessen our pain or give us something it is too painful to consider living without. Sometimes we even convince ourselves that up is down and wrong is right. Those choices almost always have a victim. Sometimes we ourselves are the victim. Whenever we turn to sin to solve our problems or broken hearts, God becomes the victim. We always sin against God when we harm ourselves or others.

We do not always run toward the moral evils when we are in pain. Sometimes we run in the equally destructive direction of perfectionism or legalism. That path strangles out patience as well and takes us right to the flashing-red-light danger zone that is at the heart of Paul's whole argument in Galatians. The Galatian church was experiencing so much change so fast that they were grasping for handholds that they believed would keep them faithful, allow them to hold onto some of their hierarchies of righteousness, and not dilute the beautiful promise given by God to Abraham and his descendants. If everybody would just submit to circumcision and the law, they reasoned, then the earth would stay beneath their feet, life would be manageable, and they would not have to be afraid that they were failing God.

Deciding that we know exactly, to the letter, in every circumstance, what God likes, dislikes, requires, and rewards, all the while making excuses for ourselves and condemning others, is poisonous soil not only to the fruit of patience but to all the other aspects as well. You cannot love and condemn. You cannot experience true joy while condemning, although sometimes one can experience the false joy of self-righteousness. You cannot experience peace while condemning. And you certainly cannot experience Spirit patience while condemning others. Judgment belongs to God, and while we are the Spirit's home and while the Spirit works through us to heal us and the world, the Spirit does not abdicate to us the responsibility to pronounce judgement on our shortsightedness.

When hardship comes and we are out of control, it can reveal all the patterns and baggage of our ego that keep us from experiencing Spirit power and grace in all things. God's intention is the transformation of pain, not the transmission of it. Scratch a sin, and you will find a wound. That is not to make excuses or to decide that the sin is justified or not really so bad after all. It is simply to say that when people sin, they show us exactly what they are afraid of.

Getting to the root of our sinful impulses is in fact the deepest and most profound repentance. After all, we cannot change what we do not see. Perhaps that was Jesus' point in the parable of the Weeds among the Wheat (Matt. 13:24–30), in which Jesus says the kingdom of heaven is like a field sown with wheat that is also sown with weeds by the enemy. As the crop grows, both the good plants and the destructive ones begin to show themselves. The man's servants ask if they should try to take out the weeds, but he says to let them grow up together so that the servants don't uproot the wrong things. When it is time for harvest, it will be obvious what is nourishing and what is worthless. It takes time for the real root of things to become inescapable.

Sometimes, of course, it is not useful or productive to wait to deal with a threat to forbearance in our soul's garden. Sometimes the ego's games are like messages whose time is ripe. Then we must look in a timely way or the weeds will completely take over.

When Robbie and I moved back to Alabama several years ago, we moved into the old home in which I grew up and in which my father was born. When the house was built in 1855, it was on a dirt road, with hitching posts out front and a barn out back for chickens and a cow. The kitchen was a separate building and the water was drawn from a well. The house had indoor plumbing and an attached kitchen well before I was born, but there was still a lot of updating to do when Robbie and I reclaimed it. We are making progress, but the one thing that we can't tackle is the barn. It is completely overgrown. The forest has reclaimed it. It is home to foxes and raccoons now, not a cow or chickens. It is invisible to the eye. If we think of the old barn as a visual icon of the soul, it is not hard to see what happens when we neglect the weeding that has to been done at the right moment. Often we lose sight of what is beneath and let the forest overtake us. Either in acting immediately or in waiting for ripe time, patience is most important at the point where it is most difficult or feels least justified.

Makrothymia grows in the soil of unity and compassion. It relies on the daily practice of recognizing and accepting our shared humanity so that we treat ourselves and others with loving-kindness (*hesed*) and wise compassion.

The compassion that is at the heart of this aspect of the Spirit's fruit is always a relationship between equals, never a hierarchy nor an attempt to fix someone or seem to do so. *Makrothymia* makes its wise choices knowing that the ones to whom we respond are siblings, just like us with all the same scars and desires and, most importantly, with a common Parent. There can be no true Spirit patience when we decide that others are less worthy of life and blessing than we are.

A conquest mentality, therefore, is a severe threat to *makrothymia*. That mentality says we must win every dispute and must never seem weak in the eyes of others. Conquest mentality sees the world as full of predators and pain, as getting worse and worse every day and in every way, so we must act, even if the enemy is nebulous and our tactics for addressing it are dramatic and ineffectual. Conquest mentality celebrates instant reflexes, hair triggers, might makes right, and the notion that we can control our hardship by obliterating the thing that scares us. *Makrothymia* does not ripen in that environment. It is not even wanted in that environment.

Often a conquest mentality includes a compulsion to repeat the past, especially a past that has been photoshopped in our minds. Scripture gives us a perfect example of this. When the people of Israel finally escaped from the bondage of Egyptian slavery and set out on their generations-long journey to the land of promised blessing, it did not take long for the shock and wonder of rescue to fade in the presence of change and uncertainty.

The wilderness was hard. It was taking decades to make what should have been a short trip. They had no idea what lie ahead, and they began to fantasize about what lay behind. "The camp followers with them had a strong craving, and the Israelites also wept again and said, 'If only we had meat to eat! We remember the fish we used to eat in Egypt for nothing, the cucumbers, the melons, the leeks, the onions, and the garlic, but now our strength is dried up, and there is nothing at all but this manna to look at'" (Num. 11:4–6).

Somehow, in all the uncertainty of their circumstance the miracle of God's daily provision paled in comparison to the memories of Egypt. When things are uncertain, we can quickly long for a past that usually never was and fight for it with all our strength. We see this in our politics today. Books that were required reading in school when I grew up are now banned under the guise of getting us back to the whitewashed glory days of life in the time in which I grew up. That mind-set does not lend itself to *makrothymia*.

The choice to endure, to refuse to retaliate, to hold our tempers, to wade in the shallows of our suffering without complaint, can leave us, too, whining for the fleshpots of Egypt in one way or another. "Let's go backward," we say. "Sure it was awful, but we knew the rules, even though we were powerless to make them. And there were melons." Waiting for something totally new to emerge can be breathtakingly hard. There are demonstrably few long fuses when what we think we want seems threatened or unduly delayed, and we fill the time with moaning, griping, and complaining.

Complaining is a form of self-justification that wastes energy at best and becomes a slippery slope to egotism at worst. Complaining itself is a form of retaliation. When we complain, we rarely practice self-observation. We often complain about others doing, or not doing, things that we ourselves do or don't do. That leads to self-righteous complaining. Whether in the form of words or actions, complaining stops Spirit fruit from ripening.

THE GIFTS OF SPIRIT PATIENCE

Late in the seventeenth century a Spanish priest named Miguel de Molinos developed a pattern of spiritual practice and mysticism that he called quietism. It might seem that this practice is rooted in patience because it rests on the abandonment of the will as a form of religious discipline. Quietism accepts things as they are without any attempts to resist or change them. The goal of quietism is to disappear into the now, like my beautiful day with Margaret. When taken to extremes, however, it can result in a total disengagement from surrounding realities. That can look like patient waiting, but in reality it can become an excuse for abandonment of self and others.

Spirit patience surely includes waiting and slowing down our impulses to respond with violence, but it is not passive in any way. Everything is a choice. The choice to not retaliate. The choice to not fight everything all the time. The choice to trust that God is up to something and will provide the needed resources at the right moment. Spirit patience has no cowardice in it and very little self-preservation. It is all about mercy, compassion, emotional control, and the decision to release expectation, need, and regret.

But what if what we are facing needs to be addressed? Does Spirit patience mean that we don't confront injustice? Does it mean that we accept what is and train ourselves to become content with it, blind to it, when it is downright awful? Of course not!

Spirit patience is concentrated strength used in love at the right time for the right reasons. While Jesus tenderly showed patience in the Garden of Gethsemane, he had already turned over the tables in the temple, let the animals go, and chased the corrupt businessmen from the place with a homemade whip. Patience is not a convenient excuse for inaction. It is a power for love in action according to God's timing. It allows us to act as God would act, when we are led in love to act. It gives us the capacity to withstand hardship, particularly hardship associated with injustice and oppression, with dignity, grace, wisdom, and power and without retaliation, despair, or desperation that can lead to damaging action.

Spirit patience slows us down and allows us to make choices rather than to be controlled by emotional reactions. In the 1970s when I was in college, my father (a state prosecutor, then judge) was the victim of an assassination attempt by a car bombing in our driveway. Mercifully he survived, but in those first moments we did not know whether he would. I remember well the taste of the explosive in my mouth. I remember the tremble in my skin as I was awakened from sleep by the blast. The consequences still linger for me. I sometimes still react physically when I hear loud noises or explosions on TV.

It was worse for my mother, who was in the car at the time but was uninjured. In those early days, we did not know who had planted the bomb or why. Was it retaliation for some sentence Daddy handed down from the bench? Was it political? Was it to prevent a ruling? We did not know. Officers from the Bureau of Alcohol, Tobacco and Firearms urged me to stay with neighbors and not to be alone.

Mom stayed on a cot in Daddy's hospital room. In those long traumatic nights, she slept little. Instead she filled her mind with detailed plans for revenge. She imagined just what she would do to the perpetrator when one was caught. This went on for days. She began to unravel even as Daddy was beginning to heal. Gradually she realized that she, too, had been assaulted and that she would not heal until she released the natural inclination to want to wound in kind. When that began to happen, she began to sleep and the journey to wholeness truly began for her. Even though the case was never officially closed and no perpetrators were ever tried, she lost the urge for revenge. Spirit's fruit of the long fuse ripened in her, and the Spirit did what only the Spirit can do in dire circumstances.

Patience protects us from retaliation that is out of proportion and not in our best interests. Can you even imagine how awful it would have been if my mom had acted on those early murderous feelings? Can you imagine how awful it would be if you acted on all your own first impulses? If we choose to act on the first flush of our feelings when we are wronged, it will not, as we may think, somehow put things right or balance some cosmic scale. It will only lower us to the level of the one who harmed us and add to the sum total of pain and misery in the world.

The gift of the long fuse allows us to slow down, to breathe, to take control of our emotions, and to ask a different set of questions. It is no longer, How can I retaliate? Rather, we ask, What are my real values, and how do I live them in these circumstances? When patience ripens in us, we find that we naturally give up the option to respond in kind to every wound.

Practicing the fruit of the long fuse, over time, also eliminates wasteful destruction of our well-being from nursing our slights and holding grudges. We gradually find that we no longer dwell on the flaws of others or the pains those flaws have dealt us. To nurture patience, we choose not to nurse our grievances. Rather, we put our energy into that which builds up, helps us see clearly, and act in ways that are righteous and uplifting. This Spirit quality allows us to tap into the power that lies beneath our pain to endure and to thrive.

CONCLUSION

Patience is the Spirit-given capacity to choose not to fight back, even against our own pain. It teaches us that there are right moments and right responses. It is rooted in a trust that whatever we are called on to face, it is not beyond the power of God to sustain us, heal us, and use us. This is particularly true when we face difficulties as a result of our faith and the values that faith calls forth. Spirit patience reminds us that we can't numb our pain by denying it. We cannot numb our pain by lashing out at those who cause it. We cannot defang our fears by sinking into legalism or any kind of numbing sin. Sin itself is an avoidance tactic. It is never an effective strategy to get what we want or to not get what we don't want.

On that day sitting on a bench with my friend, there was not enough tea in Mississippi to numb me to what I wanted to fight against: my friend Margaret was dying. There was not a cool enough breeze to make chemo work if it would not. On the day when I picked up pieces of my father's legs from our driveway, all the photoshopping of that horror would never erase the truth of it. Long-suffering, the capacity to endure, without violence, is what we need when things come apart. It will not ripen in an environment of denial. Only awareness, slowing down, taking the long view of compassion, has the power to feed the warmhearted patience that is the heartbeat of God. It is only that heartbeat, hidden beneath our own, that brings patience to fruit.

A WEEK TO TEND PATIENCE

Day One: "Look, now is the acceptable time; look, now is the day of salvation! We are putting no obstacle in anyone's way, so that no fault may be found with our ministry, but as servants of God we have commended ourselves in every way: in great endurance . . . ; in purity, knowledge, patience, kindness, holiness of spirit. . . ." (2 Cor. 6:2b–6). Paul is writing to a church in trouble. They are fighting about almost everything. In this section, he is trying to help them, and us, see that the way we behave and treat one another is our witness. That is how the truth of Christ will be judged by those we seek to reach. If we are impatient with and unkind toward others, then the whole of our message is undercut. Who has tested your patience this week? Have you found yourself speaking sharply to anyone, especially in the presence of others? Ask God to fill you with forgiveness and patience in your interactions. Ask also for an awareness of the wonderful responsibility you have as a Christian to make the faith look good. When you are irritated, take a moment to breathe and ask yourself how your response will make Christ look.

Day Two: "I, therefore, the prisoner in the Lord, beg you to walk in a manner worthy of the calling to which you have been called, with all humility and gentleness, with patience, bearing with one another in love, making every effort to maintain the unity of the Spirit in the bond of peace" (Eph. 4:1–3). The author of Ephesians recognizes that the way we treat each other not only is a threat to the spread of the gospel but also can tear apart the believing community as well. There can be no unity in the body without qualities of character like patience. What are the things about which you have the shortest fuse? What things in the life of the church do you think should have been taken care of yesterday? What seems to trigger your impatience most? When you feel impatient with others, what thoughts do you have about them? Ask God to help you replace those negative feelings toward others with genuine understanding and compassion. Look for ways to change your thoughts toward those who irritate you.

Day Three: "May you be made strong with all the strength that comes from his glorious power, so that you may have all endurance and patience, joyfully giving thanks to the Father, who has enabled you to share in the inheritance of the saints in the light" (Col. 1:11–12). Patience is necessary to live with joy, endurance, strength, and power. How powerful and joyful do you feel when you give in to impatience? Not very, I suspect. We all have feelings of impatience. We don't have to eradicate them. Rather, we transform them and replace them with the Spirit's gift of patience. Notice any times that you feel rushed, any times that you do not have room for interruptions. What is motivating you at those times? Often you will find that your motivator is not love. When you find yourself feeling irritable, try thinking of something joyful instead. For example, if you catch yourself thinking something like, "I can't believe she is keeping me waiting this way!" Think instead, "I am overjoyed to have a moment on my own." Or, "The anticipation of our visit is just as sweet as the time together." Ask God to transform your impatience into a time of prayer.

Day Four: "As God's chosen ones, holy and beloved, clothe yourselves with compassion, kindness, humility, meekness, and patience" (Col. 3:12). In this verse, we see that while patience is a free gift of the Spirit, it is also something that we can pick up and put down, put on or take off, just like a sweater or a jacket. Today, notice any times that you feel held back or that your timing is tampered with. When you begin to react negatively, visualize yourself putting on the sweater of patience. Remind yourself that you are not in danger, that you can control your responses to situations. Ask God to surround you with patience today as your protective covering. Nothing can get to you or threaten to undo you through that marvelous cloak of God's own patience.

Day Five: "And we want each one of you to show the same diligence so as to realize the full assurance of hope to the very end, so that you may not become sluggish but imitators of those who through faith and patience inherit the promises" (Heb. 6:11–12). What amazing verses these are! The author links patience with faith as the vehicles through which we attain all that God promises to us. Faith simply means trust. Patience in this instance means more than having a long fuse. It also means to have confidence in God's timing and not to become impatient with God. Have you ever felt impatient with God? Can you think of a time when you thought God should do something for you and it didn't happen as you wanted or when you wanted? This verse tells us that trusting in God's ways and God's timing is necessary for us to receive the things God longs to give us. Today, as many times as you can think of it, say this prayer, "God, I trust that your timing is perfect. Nothing can shake me, because I am right where you want me to be."

Day Six: "Brothers and sisters, do not grumble against one another, so that you may not be judged. See, the Judge is standing at the doors! As an example of suffering and patience, brothers and sisters, take the prophets who spoke in the name of the Lord" (Jas. 5:9–10). James recognizes that grumbling is deadly to community, and he looks to the lives of the prophets as examples of waiting on the Lord. One of his points is that we are to model our behavior toward others on the way the holy ones treated the Lord. Have you behaved toward anyone this week in a way that you would not like to behave toward God? Have you said anything to or about another that you would not like to say to or about God? Have you grumbled and complained about anyone? Ask God to bring to mind any instances of this behavior and to forgive you. Ask God to help you to see Christ in every person and to treat each one as you would Jesus.

Questions for Reflection and Discussion

1. When you think of patience as having a supernaturally long fuse, who are some of the people you know who demonstrate that quality?
2. What makes it difficult for you to experience patience in your everyday life? *uncertainty*
3. How do you see our culture fueling impatience? What can you do to keep your balance in these retaliatory times?
4. How do you keep the balance *prayer & peace* of patience and action? How do you know when each one is called for?
5. Was there anything surprising to you in this chapter? How so?

CHAPTER 6

TENDING THE
SHOOTS OF KINDNESS

*There are two ways of spreading light: to be the
candle or the mirror that reflects it.*
— Edith Wharton

It was a stormy March night in Alabama when, more
than forty years ago, I found myself in the hospital in
Tuscaloosa watching tornadoes jump the Black Warrior
River and lift over the specialty care unit where I lay. I was
twenty-one, desperately ill, and mostly oblivious to how
serious the situation was. I had been throwing blood clots
to my lungs for several days. Specialists from as far away
as Boston who had been consulted recommended everything from amputation of my leg to removal of my lung.
My local doctors were reluctant to do those surgeries,
in part because I was so young and in part because they
thought I was too unstable to withstand the operation.

That particular night my doctor explained to me what
was happening by drawing a picture of my lungs on the back
of his prescription pad. He said that if things continued as

they were going, he did not think I would survive the night. My friends came in to say their good-byes. When they had all shuffled back to their dorms or set up camp in the waiting room to weather the storm with me amid textbooks and flattened sacks of Cheetos, the hospital lost power. Emergency generators were employed. The light was gray and eerie. I was too fragile to move to the bed-lined corridor, so a nervous nurse put pillows by my head in case of flying glass.

At that point, my doctor sat down next to me. He pulled a pocket New Testament and Psalms from his lab coat and in the dim light read psalms to me. All night. As the storm intensified outside and the clots swirled like tornadoes inside, he sat and read the psalms.

I drifted in and out of his words while rubbing my thumb rhythmically across and down the gold-embossed cross on the Bible I received from my church when I was in third grade. All night, that young resident — a Presbyterian elder, I later learned — sat there and read the words of Scripture. Why did he do that? Was it his job? Not really. Was he afraid? Was I about to be the first patient he lost? I do not know. But what I do know is that in that dark room on that stormy night, that young man's faith erupted into kindness I will never forget. I have no doubt that the power of his faith-filled kindness played a role in my survival. Spirit kindness is love gathering the courage to choose the less-trodden path. It is the choice to do whatever one can to be a messenger of God's tender mercy.

Spirit kindness arises from the way we see the world. If we see the world as teeming with rivers of grace, as my young doctor did, kindness naturally flows from us. If we see that what is happening in heaven is also happening on earth in the here and now, kindness bubbles up like a spring from a source of wonder and trust deep within us. When we see all creation as one intricate, inextricable whole that is filled with the goodness of God, gradually we begin to realize that how we do anything is how we do everything, and how we think about anything is how we come to think about everything. Then, kindness becomes unavoidable; and unkindness, unthinkable.

KINDNESS IN THE BIBLE

In the Hebrew Scriptures, the word ordinarily translated as kindness is *hesed*. We explored that word in chapter 5. It means to commit to someone or something. It means to display devotion without conditions.

When I first began researching the word for kindness in my Hebrew concordance, I made a mistake. I shifted a number, and it took me to a rarely used Hebrew word usually translated as "prominent," stemming from a root that means "full or plentiful breasts." Now, while that is *not* the word used for kindness, sometimes the Spirit can take us into unexpected places through our mistakes: kindness is indeed like a nursing mother who never fails to support and nourish her beloved child. As the prophet Isaiah says, "Can a woman forget her nursing child or show no compassion for the child of her womb?" (Isa. 49:15).

This quote from Isaiah comes from a passage of hope and promise. It is intended to encourage a weary people to trust that God will never forsake them. God will show *hesed* to them. God will take them to the fullness of God's own breast. God's steadfast love, kindness, and provision are filled with this parental tenderness and wisdom.

In the closing chapter of Proverbs, the writer ends his collection of spiritual wisdom with the description of a worthy woman. He describes an industrious person who is strong, hardworking, tender, and unafraid. In 31:26 the writer tells us that when she speaks, she is full of wisdom, and kindness (*hesed*) is always on her tongue. In that way she mirrors God, who is always trustworthy, strong, capable, fearless, beautiful, wise, kind, and working day and night for the good of the beloved. Throughout the many hardships and defeats that Israel endured, that image of steadfast loving-kindness sustained them. Even when the thunders rumbled and God's wrath was kindled, God's loving-kindness always got the last word.

In the New Testament, the word we translate as "kindness" in Galatians 5:22, *chrestotes*, arises from these bedrock beliefs in God's unshakable kindness and mercy. *Chrestotes* is rendered in a number of ways. In some instances, it is translated as "goodness." Indeed, it has similarities with the word Paul uses next in his list of the fruit of the Spirit, often translated as "goodness," but it is a little different. *Chrestotes* doesn't refer to being sweet and not hurting people's feelings. It is more substantial than that. It means to be gracious, to find goodness easy, to display integrity, to be drawn to excellence in personal behavior, and to be quick to support excellence in others. At its heart, *chrestotes* is compassionate and useful. To live out of Spirit kindness is to be of service, especially when it would be easier not to be.

In Luke 6, Jesus widens the lens through which we view kindness. After castigating the hypocrites for their hatred and greed in the boldest possible way, he goes on to tell them that they are to love their enemies, bless those who curse them, and pray for those who abuse them. He crowns his argument by reminding them that a defining quality of God is kindness (*chrestotes*) and that kindness is extended not just to the upright but also to "the ungrateful and the wicked" (v. 35). Because God is steadfastly kind, those who follow God are also to be steadfastly kind. It is to apply to all. Kindness is to be characteristic of how God's people relate to loved ones, faith family, strangers, and enemies. No one lies outside the embrace of God's kindness or our own.

The early Christian community understood that the ultimate kindness of God was displayed in the life, death, and resurrection of Jesus. Therefore, living a Christlike life must include genuine kindness, courage, and sacrifice. Illustrating this point in Colossians 3:12, the author tells us that we are to clothe ourselves with kindness. It is to be what people first see in us. Far from being a mere facade, looking like Jesus on the outside requires that we look like Jesus on the inside. Actions of Spirit kindness require congruence between the Spirit who resides within us and the actions we take in the world. We are to be lovingly useful and to display what being lovingly useful looks like in everyday life, not as actors who learn their lines for reward, but because we are God's children, adopted in Christ and therefore urged to reflect God in personal transformation and serviceable kindness.

TENDING THE SPIRIT'S KINDNESS IN OUR LIVES

Spirit kindness is incarnational at core. It connects heart-to-heart, in groans too deep for words, as the apostle Paul puts it. Whether it is Pooh and Piglet going to sit with the dispirited Eeyore in the children's book *Winnie the Pooh*, or Sam insisting on going with Frodo into the dangerous waters in *The Lord of the Rings* trilogy, we experience the power of kindness in the concrete experiences of human relationships. There are infinite ways that we can share kindness in daily life. The following are a few examples.

Kindness as Silent Presence

Sometimes the greatest kindness is sitting with someone in their pain. Pastor Kim Vanbrimmer told me a story from a sorrowful time in her life. "Years ago," she says, "in my former parish, my grandfather had been sick, and my friends and colleagues knew that he was in his final days. The day I got the call from my mom, I sat on the bench in front of the sanctuary and just cried. Pastor Jody Beth Melton was just arriving. She saw me crying, came over, and sat down next to me. She gently put an arm around me, and said, 'Don't stop crying.' We just sat there for a few minutes, with no expectation from her for me to talk, no platitudes, just the comfort of a friend who let me grieve. It was so kind. I'll never forget it." Sitting quietly with a friend in grief is a powerful demonstration of God's incarnational presence in every circumstance. Jody Beth did not tell Kim to buck up. She did not tell her that everything would be all right. With her silent presence, she acknowledged the loss too deep for words and demonstrated that Kim was honored for her grief and accompanied in it. In silent presence, the silence itself becomes kindness, when words can often distract or harm.

This kind of silent presence is simple but not passive. Rather, it is quite active. It captures the graciousness at the heart of Spirit kindness especially well when we are in situations in which we are overwhelmed and do not know the circumstances or values of others involved. In situations like that, a metaphorical cup of cool water in Jesus' name can change everything.

I experienced silence as kindness once during a difficult time in my own life. In an effort to find my way, I took a silent retreat at a Jesuit monastery a few miles from my home. Each day when I arrived back in my little cell after a silent breakfast with the brothers, I found my bed made and a small object left on my desk. One day it was a beautiful twig with a tiny pine cone. Another day it was a small rock with a line of sparkling quartz. One day it was a blue jay feather. The brothers and I never spoke a word to one another. I never knew even one name or what stories brought them to that life. All they knew about me was that I was a Presbyterian pastor seeking the restorative power of the Spirit. We came from different traditions and had different expectations of life and faith. Yet every morning I received an offering of Spirit kindness with which to ground my silence in a gracious presence that needed no words and was actually enhanced by their absence.

Developing comfort with holy silence is often a counter-cultural practice these days when we hold our smartphones most of our waking hours and live with the constant distraction of banner ads, beeps, and tweets. When we silence all of that, we can feel a mix of discomfort and anxiety. What if we miss something important? What do we do with the silence? Who are we really when the bells silence and we are left to sit with our own souls for a moment? It can be unnerving, and unless we are willing to weather the discomfort, we will not experience the gracious kindness of God in those quiet moments.

In the moments when silence is particularly terrifying— when the phone doesn't ring for weeks after the biopsy, when a loved one won't talk about what is troubling him, when we pray for guidance and find none—we often thrash about looking for ways to fix whatever is troubling us or a loved one. Developing comfort with silence and not having all the answers is not easy. For some of us, it requires new spiritual skills of focus and calming breathing. It requires the best of us and a fair amount of discipline, but it is worth it. Holy silence creates space for the Spirit's garden in our souls, like good potting soil in which the everlasting kindness of the Spirit's presence within rises, blossoms, and bears fruit.

Kindness as Noticing

Spirit kindness also ripens in the simple act of noticing other people and recognizing them as fully human, as our siblings on the earth. Spirit kindness keeps its eyes and hearts tuned to the edges, for there are endless opportunities to offer kindness there.

My friend Harriett lost her son in an automobile accident shortly before his sixteenth birthday. She shares, "When David died, I was sending thank-you notes for all the many acts of kindness we received. I came across a flower arrangement that had no name or address on it and, not wanting to leave anyone out, I called the florist to see if they might help me. The florist informed me that the person did not want to be identified. When I explained the reason I wanted the information, the florist still would not give me a name but did reveal that the person who sent the flowers was one of my son's classmates, a big girl who generally felt left out and unpopular. She said that my son had made her feel special and accepted, and she wanted to do something nice for him. I have never been so proud of David in my life." We don't know exactly what David did. Did he smile at her in the hall? Pick her for his team in gym class? Invite her to sit with him and his friends at lunch? Offer her a lift home from school? It could have been any of those things or any small act of recognizing another human being who was in pain and feeling isolated. What is clear is that he noticed her, and somehow simply being seen and treated kindly touched her deeply.

Spirit kindness such as this can be a conduit of healing grace that is powerful enough to change a life. Kindness is not merely a momentary anesthetic. It is medicine from heaven itself. It is a reminder that we are each noticed by God, whose eye is on the sparrow, the least of these, and even our own hurting selves. To manifest Spirit kindness is to point people toward the deepest truths about themselves and their beloved status. Did David intend to do that or even know that he was doing that? It doesn't matter. The Spirit moved him and used him just as the Spirit will move and use each of us when we are brave enough to tend the garden of kindness.

Kindness as noticing always invites us to broaden our vision. Being kind is like living with a wide-angle lens in our awareness. No one is outside the view of one who is maturing in kindness. A colleague, Thom M. Shuman, illustrates this point with a story about his son who is mentally and developmentally disabled. In the ways of kindness, however, he is marvelously able. Thom recounts that when his son was six years old, his mom and he were at a park for a picnic and outing. As they sat at the picnic table, Teddy noticed an obviously homeless person sitting on a nearby bench. Teddy went over and sat on the bench and handed half his sandwich to his new friend. "They enjoyed that feast in companionable silence and then went their separate ways." What strikes me in that poignant story is that Spirit kindness revealed in simply noticing another person is sacramental. In Teddy noticing the other person and immediately going to share a meal with them, heaven seemed to open and a peanut butter and jelly sandwich torn in two became an outward and visible sign of an inward and spiritual grace. Distinctions and privileges became, for a moment, meaningless, just as they do when we approach the sacrament in our churches. The kindness of noticing sees much more than station or situation. It sees more than pain or joy. Spirit kindness sees commonality, one humanity, one sandwich, one loaf, broken and shared.

Sadly, sometimes kindness is denied and grace dammed up by our choice not to see others in their full humanity. It is not as simple as missing opportunities for kindness because we avert our eyes from those who call us out of our comfort zones. Sometimes we see those in need of kindness but don't see them as being enough like us to deserve it. Spirit kindness has no category of deserving. Did any of us deserve God's kindness? Obviously not. Did any of us contribute to the situations that left us so in need of God's kindness? Obviously. Blindness to the full humanity of others will always stunt the growth of Spirit kindness. Opening our eyes to the deeply incarnational nature of our faith will result in Spirit kindness that both changes lives and demonstrates the graciousness of God.

Kindness as Lifting Up Others

Kindness elevates the spirit and helps us have the confidence that we need to face situations that are hard for us. It gives us the opportunity to see our situations and ourselves differently. When someone offers us kindness, we can begin to imagine a reality that is bigger and truer than our fears.

As a young child, I was ill much of the time. I missed a lot of school, and when I was in school, I carried a secret fear that all the other kids knew something that I had missed. In the second grade, our class had to take achievement tests. I remember it vividly; it was hot and the whole school smelled of the chemical compound that was spread on the floors for sanitation. I was utterly terrified of those tests. I was wheezing from the compound and the anxiety. My favorite orange dress with yellow circles on it did nothing to boost my esteem.

As the tests were distributed face down on each individual desk, I looked around at my friends. They all looked as if they did not have a care in the world. I was sure I would fail. Our teacher explained the process and told us to begin. Before I began the test, I crept up to her desk and whispered, "May I ask Debbie if there are words I don't understand?" "No, Genie," she said. "You know everything you need to know. You can do this. Let's show them!" I don't remember taking the test, but the kind words of that teacher were Spirit kisses to me.

Spirit kindness has the capacity to heal our self-esteem and reframe our understanding of who we are and what we are capable of doing. When that teacher told me I knew what I needed to know, I tentatively began to believe her. For a moment, I was no longer the sick kid who had missed so much. I was the kid who knew enough and had an ally to boot. Her long-ago kind affirmation has remained with me, as Spirit kindness does, in many of the other tests of my life. I have learned to see myself not as feeble and unprepared but as enough for situations as they arise. When I feel challenged beyond what I fear my meager abilities to be, I hear these words as if coming from Spirit's own inner kindness.

That kind of elevating kindness can reframe how we see ourselves and others. It also sets courage in motion in the human heart. It is a way for the Spirit to answer prayers. It can even, as Isaiah puts it in his vision of the return of the exiles to Zion, "strengthen the weak hands and make firm the feeble knees" (35:3).

Kindness as Courage

Spirit kindness is not limited to silent presence, sacramental noticing, encouraging words, or small sacrifices. Like Spirit herself, kindness can also be fierce. While the goodness we will explore in the next chapter is more confrontational than Spirit kindness, still *chrestotes* is the sort of kindness that works itself out boldly and actively in groups, structures, and institutions. It is not possible to be kind and do nothing in the presence of oppression, violence, and brutality. What passes for kindness in those circumstances is like trying to put a Band-Aid on an amputated limb. In the presence of the near-daily carnage of gun violence in the United States, for example, inaction is both unkind and inexcusable. We may debate exactly what actions must be taken and in what order, but when janitors, teachers, and nine-year-olds are gunned down in classrooms, debate is at best luxurious and at worst thinly disguised cowardice. Kindness and cowardice cannot occupy the same space at the same time.

The love that is the deep root of kindness is not self-serving, and cowardice always is. To try to be kind while we turn a blind eye to any oppression or violence and move on to the next news cycle is a dereliction of duty in the kingdom of God. Kindness, like *agape,* always moves out on behalf of those who are in pain, especially the helpless who crumble under the boot of the powerful. We do not wait for complete knowledge in order to act in kindness. We simply get out of the Spirit's way and offer our hearts, minds, bodies, and energies to be the hands and feet of God, who always seeks to free, heal, and restore. If we are not working in that direction, then we cannot claim to be kind.

WEEDS IN THE
GARDEN OF KINDNESS

As we have considered a few of the many ways Spirit kindness manifests, some of the weeds that keep kindness from maturing have become obvious: Speaking when words can only harm. The inability to bear silence. Narrowing whom we allow ourselves to see. Attaching the foreign concept of deserving as a litmus test for kindness. Tearing others down instead of lifting them up. Those are potent and just a beginning.

Self-serving motivation that results from trying to seem kind in order to somehow meet our own needs, without the inner transformation into actually being kind, is another stealthy weed that weakens kindness. Spirit kindness is focused on others and cannot be counterfeit. We can say all the right words but still not emit the transformative power of kindness. Kind words or actions that arise as a thinly disguised need to be loved, or seen as special, secure, or worthy of approval, cannot be called Spirit kindness. True Spirit kindness is never manipulative. Any hint of that is a destructive weed. Spirit kindness is not offered to gain a particular response or benefit for the one offering it. It is not controlling or fixated on a particular outcome. Kindness wants to shower love with words, actions, prayers, and tenderness that help others know just how deeply loved they are.

We certainly may choose to try to be kind as a spiritual discipline. We may even do wonderful-seeming actions that may be used by God to help people. The paradox is that the Spirit can use even our mixed motives for good for ourselves and others. When motivated by our maturing love and the Spirit's direction, trying itself becomes an act of kindness to our own souls, gradually moving us from *doing* kindness to naturally being kind. Gradually our internal thoughts and motivations will begin to align with those of the Spirit who plants and tends the garden within us.

Showing gracious kindness to ourselves as we seek to mature in kindness is sometimes harder than showing kindness to others. Self-harm, whether emotional or physical, is a weed that makes kindness if not impossible at least shallow and needy. To accept the Spirit's kindness toward us and mature it within us often requires unlearning decades-old patterns of behavior and thought. That kind of weed pulling takes time and persistence. It requires repentance and making new choices. For example, maybe we tear ourselves down in our thoughts, saying such things as "I'm fat," "I'm too old," "I'm too young," "I'm a failure," "I'm defective," "I'm unlovable." In order to live from Spirit kindness, we need to recognize that those thoughts are lies. That is not how God sees us at all. Those lies cause harm, and God does not cause us harm.

To begin to ripen Spirit kindness, when we are unkind to ourselves, we start by refusing to compare ourselves to some arbitrary standard that comes from our culture or our experience but not from the tender mercy of God. We can then decide to replace harming thoughts with true thoughts like, "I am beloved of God. I have been made whole and perfected in Christ." This is not puffing ourselves up or stoking our egos. This is the truth.

With whatever clever words we use to disguise it, when we offer hate toward ourselves, we will quickly find it impossible to offer true kindness to another. Why? Because in that offering of kindness we will always be looking for an antidote to our own wounds. Then the other becomes an object through whose reactions we hope to drown out the inner barrage of our own poor self-esteem. To truly mature, kindness requires inner healing of guilt, shame, or self-talk that keeps us focused on ourselves. Negative self-talk only redirects any energy we might have to offer kindness in our world to trying to heal a wound we scratch the scab off of again and again and again.

Another weed in kindness's patch is offering kindness in a way that we would want to receive it rather than in a way that the other actually desires it. Again, doing for another what we think they want or should want makes us the referent and arbiter of our actions. It is important to remember that not everything we intend as kindness will be received as kindness. The receiver always gets to decide. My friend Pat says that there is a platinum rule that trumps even the Golden Rule of "do to others as you would have them do to you." Her platinum rule is "do to others as they would have you do to them."

Actions that we find loving may not seem loving to another. A friend tells the story of how, early in her marriage, she and her husband wrestled with this as they learned to care for each other when ill. She wanted to be checked on when ill, and he wanted to be left alone. At first, he left her alone, and she felt unloved. She constantly checked on him, and he felt irritated. Quickly they learned that the way to be kind is to set aside our own expectations and offer what the other truly needs, not what we think they need because it is what we need.

On a much larger scale, we can see the ramifications of not learning this respectful form of kindness in the damage done to peoples and cultures through paternalistic missionary endeavors born of colonialism. Even what we perceive as altruism can sometimes cripple or disrespect those we want to help. Spirit kindness is respectful and always takes others' desires into account.

Trying to fix what is not ours to fix is another weed in the Spirit's garden of kindness. As we see in the story of Job and his well-meaning but ultimately hurtful friends, sometimes we can damage our expressions of kindness in times of grief or turmoil by trying to too quickly fix the situation, find a way out, or resort to platitudes that diminish the other's pain. When Job's friends saw the depths of the grief and loss surrounding Job, they came to see him. But their visit was diagnostic in nature. Why did this happen? What did you do to cause your problems? How can you fix it? In their discomfort with the apparent randomness of Job's downfall, they were not trying to help Job. They were trying to reestablish their own sense of equilibrium in the face of a confounding situation. Their presence was more about them than their friend. Unkindness may not have been the intent, but it was the result.

Sometimes, to be kind, we have to be willing to sit in a situation that makes us uncomfortable, in which we do not have the answers. We have to sit and stay, not run from our feelings of inadequacy and not try to stanch those feelings with old wisdom that is shallow and potentially shaming. To try to fix another's situation, or especially their emotions, when what we really want is to be comfortable ourselves is a powerful weed in kindness's garden.

While it can be unkind to try to fix others inappropriately, refusing to take responsibility for what we can and must try to fix is unkind and will strangle out our impulses to kindness eventually. Our response to the earth itself is a prime example of this. Creation is full of the tender mercies of God, and each day, the entire created order asks for that mercy to be returned to it. When the planet quivers in pain due to humans' unkind and greedy choices, we ourselves feel the results, as do our children and grandchildren who will have to live on a hurting land. We may shrug our shoulders and wonder what we can do. We may toss the needed actions into God's court alone and ask for miracles to overcome our own global actions and inactions. When we ask for a miracle to remedy our environmental crisis and every other injustice plaguing humanity, we can be assured that we will receive it. The miracle needed is us, our hands, our feet, our voices. Again I hear my second-grade teacher saying, "You know everything you need to know. You can do this. Let's show them."

CONCLUSION

Spirit kindness is infinitely nuanced and creative. We know it by its transforming results in our lives and world. It flourishes in compassionate relationships. It ripens in holy silence. It sees and cherishes all creatures. It fiercely moves with graciousness and forgiveness. It reframes a haunting, negative narrative into one of hope and growth. It is redemptive and endlessly powerful. It is also easily strangled out by fear, discomfort, faulty assumptions, and self-judgment. Still, it cannot be eradicated, even if it is sometimes buried or dormant. Kindness is at the core of the human experience because it is at the heart of the very nature of God.

It may seem daunting to think about living with the Spirit's bountiful kindness toward ourselves, others, and creation itself. And yet that is our birthright. We were created by kindness. We are redeemed by kindness. We live by kindness. The Spirit constantly offers reminders of what kindness that flows from the core of being looks like: a precious memory that arises at the right moment, or the perfect book showing up in your Facebook feed, or the song of the Carolina wren when your spirits flag. The Spirit is constantly kind and looking for hearts capable of understanding kindness and transmitting it.

I believe that the angels and the ancestors surround us with kindness all the time. When we find it hard to be kind, when we lack courage, when we have been hurt and want to wound in kind or find someone to blame, we can still trust that we are constantly surrounded by a great cloud of witnesses (Heb. 12:1) who are cheering us on, celebrating our halting steps forward, and cheering all the louder when we fall and have the courage to rise and try again. If we stop and are willing to listen, we will hear their voices. We will feel their loving energy. We will realize that we are part of something eternally kind. We are never alone in striving to pull out the weeds of hatred, violence, oppression, self-service, fractured self-esteem, greed, or apathy that can so easily strangle out the shoots of kindness in our lives and in the whole created order. As Frances Hodgson Burnett wrote in *Little Lord Fauntleroy*, "Nothing in the world is so strong as a kind heart."[8]

A WEEK FOR
TENDING KINDNESS

Day One: "Blessed be he by the LORD, whose kindness has not forsaken the living or the dead!" (Ruth 2:20). Throughout the day, ask God to help you notice the times when someone shows you kindness, whether it is the checker at the grocery store or a friend or family member. Don't focus on the moments of unkindness or disrespect. Let those go! At bedtime, jot down a few of the moments of kindness you received and noticed today and thank God for them.

Day Two: "Those who withhold kindness from a friend forsake the fear of the Almighty" (Job 6:14). Notice today the opportunities to be kind that you did not take. What do you think led you to neglect those opportunities? At bedtime, take a moment to list those moments, and let them be the basis of your prayer of confession. Ask God to provide more opportunities for kindness tomorrow. Give no thought or energy to the ways others could have been more kind to you. You cannot change that, but you can change you. Jot down a word about those missed opportunities and thank God that a new day will bring you more chances.

Day Three: "Whoever pursues righteousness and kindness will find life and honor" (Prov. 21:21). Reflect today on how you might increase (pursue) opportunities to show kindness. Ask God to open your eyes and take you out of your comfort zone. Notice the looks around people's eyes. Say a kind word. If something irritates you, remember that most people are doing the best they can. Practice a kind word in every situation. At bedtime, survey your day. How did you seek out opportunities to be kind? In what circumstances was that most difficult?

In what situations was it impossible? Jot down the ways you went out of your way to be kind today. Note, too, any special kindnesses you received today. Thank God for loving others through your kindness and for loving you through the kindness of others.

Day Four: "For you always have the poor with you, and you can show kindness to them whenever you wish, but you will not always have me" (Mark 14:7). Reflect today on ways that you can show kindness to the poor. Ponder also the nature of true kindness. Kindness always builds up the other and connects them to a deep source of inner power. Kindness is not motivated by guilt or the need for a response. Its motivation is gratitude to God for our own blessings. At bedtime, make a list of ways that you can show kindness to the poor. Choose one way from that list as your mission for tomorrow.

Day Five: "As God's chosen ones, holy and beloved, clothe yourselves with compassion, kindness, humility, meekness, and patience. Bear with one another and, if anyone has a complaint against another, forgive each other; just as the Lord has forgiven you, so you also must forgive" (Col. 3:12–13). Notice today any people whom you have difficulty forgiving. It is hard to be consistently kind when we harbor resentment toward another or spend energy on an unforgiving heart. Ask God to help you let go of resentments so that you can have a generous heart. At bedtime, practice opening your heart to forgive. Forgiving does not mean saying that what happened was OK. If it had been OK, you wouldn't need to forgive. Nor does it mean that you have to reopen the relationship if it is not safe or prudent to do so. Forgiveness just frees up your heart to live more bountifully and kindly. If this is too hard, be kind to yourself and give yourself more time. Thank God for giving you the courage to start.

Day Six: "All have turned aside; together they have become worthless; there is no one who shows kindness; there is not even one" (Rom. 3:12). Today reflect on the importance of kindness and its scarcity in your life and in the world. Kindness is at the heart of righteousness. Ponder how you may be able to recover a deep and abiding spirit of kindness in your life. At bedtime, make a promise to God that you will seek Christ more every day. Tell God how much you yearn to be kind and to spread the spirit of kindness in your life, in your church, and in the world. Ask God to show you ways that God wants to use you to spread kindness. Take a moment to jot down every instance where you have noticed kindness today. Pray for that kindness to multiply like the stars in the heaven.

Questions for Reflection and Discussion

1. How have you experienced God's kindness toward you this week? In what form did that kindness come?
2. Neuroscientists tell us that acts of kindness release endorphins, neurotransmitters that alleviate pain and lower blood pressure. God has designed our bodies to benefit from genuine kindness both when we receive it and when we offer it. Kindness is God's medicine. Have you ever experienced a kindness high? Share the story with your group.
3. Kindness can be diluted by greed and fear. What do you see as obstacles to kindness in our world?
4. God's kindness is a wide land without borders. None are excluded. Do you see people or groups whom others exclude from kindness and God's wide mercy? Why do you think this happens?

5. What relationship, if any, do you see between kindness and sin? How do you respond to the often-heard statement "Love the sinner; hate the sin" in light of Spirit kindness?
6. I suggested in this chapter that deserving or worthiness is not a category of the Spirit's thought. How do you respond to that? Is there anything inside you that resists that radical kind of grace? Talk this over as a group.

Handwritten note: He has told you, O man, what is good, and what does the Lord require of you but to act justly, love mercy + walk humbly w/ your God. Mic 6:8

CHAPTER 7

—— ⟨∞⟩ ——

TENDING THE
SHOOTS OF GOODNESS

> *Do all the good you can, by all the means you*
> *can, in all the ways you can, in all the places you*
> *can, at all the times you can, to all the people you*
> *can, as long as ever you can.*
>
> —John Wesley

I was eleven years old the night the call came. As president of the local Beatles fan club, I had spent the day making giant flowers out of multicolored crepe paper, cutting out Beatles pictures from *Sixteen* magazine, and planning the agenda for our next meeting. The album *Help!* had just been released, and our club needed to vote on our favorite tracks. I was aware, in a vague sort of way, of events taking place forty miles away in a town called Selma, where the now-sainted Rep. John Lewis, Dr. Martin Luther King Jr., Mrs. Amelia Boynton, and so many other famous and never-famous people were marching from the Brown Memorial Church to the state capital in Montgomery in support of voting rights.

In those days, we had one phone in the house, and I could hear the ring clearly even though I was in bed by then. My parents had been out to dinner that night. My father, who was district attorney at the time, had been on edge for days. Mama later told me that the last words Daddy said to her that night as they turned off the light were, "Thank God we got them all there alive." Then the call came, and Daddy had to head off into the night. A young civil rights worker named Viola Liuzzo had been killed ferrying marchers back to Selma after the triumphant gathering on the capitol steps.

Each time I saw Rep. John Lewis in his storied career, I thought of the day when he was beaten nearly to death by state troopers and deputized vigilantes. Whenever I saw his face, I saw the Liuzzo trial that consumed my eleventh summer and the courage it takes to put one's life on the line for goodness. I never saw Mr. Lewis without hearing him urge us to get in the way of that which is wrong, to get into trouble, *good* trouble. I hear it still as the struggle lumbers on.

The sixth aspect of Spirit's fruit described in Galatians 5 is *agathosyne*. Translated as "generosity" in the New Revised Standard Version Updated Edition of the Bible used by many churches, it is rendered as "goodness" in a number of other translations. The concept certainly contains both meanings. While the loveliness of *chrestotes* (kindness) mellows our character, *agathosyne* takes that character to the streets. *Agathosyne* is nonviolent but can be quite confrontational. When I read the word, I hear Rep. Lewis's voice saying, "You must be bold, brave, and courageous and find a way to get in the way."[9] That is goodness rising up from the core of a person.

If we gaze into the Spirit's garden with goodness in mind, we see something powerful and unmistakable. We see Spirit truth that reminds us that thoughts and prayers, while always valuable and often expressions of the Spirit's kindness and power, are not the end point. They are the beginning. Spirit goodness confronts us with the truth that if we cling to the garment of piety and do not follow with the clothes of concrete action, we are merely false teachers and whitewashed tombs. The world will instantly see that too. *Agathosyne* is goodness that makes things happen. It is a moral character that is energized and expresses itself. It is zealous for the good. It is also zealous for the truth. It is faith on its feet, moving the world toward the fullness of the values of God.

Why then the translation "generosity"? I have never been completely sure. Every translation is an interpretation. There is no getting around that. Perhaps it has to do with the fact that God's action, God's good trouble, God's taking it to the streets, is always generous. God pours out Godself, holding nothing back, hedging no bets, facing even the billy club of the cross.

GOD'S GOODNESS IN THE BIBLE

In the Hebrew Scriptures, there is one word, *tov*, that is translated as "good or goodness." It is a general word applied to God, people, situations, the land, and its creatures. It means to be pleasant, beneficial, favorable, cheerful, and to do good, to adorn, to cheer up. It sometimes refers to something being morally good. More often, though, the words "righteousness," "justice," or even "uprightness" are used in those circumstances.

In the Old Testament, God's goodness consists of God's loving-kindness, mercy, direction, and redemption. God displays God's goodness in an *agathosyne* way when God parts the Red Sea to lead the people out of bondage into promised blessing. God displays God's goodness in the entirety of creation that is ordered so carefully and generously, and after each creation, "God saw that it was *tov*."

God displays God's goodness and perfection in the gift of the Law and in the means of grace that the sacrificial system allows as a way to make up for sinful choices. In Psalm 73:28, God's simple nearness is all the goodness the psalmist desires. God is *tov*, and God does *tov*.

In the New Testament, three different words are translated as goodness. One is *chrestotes*, the word we examined in the previous chapter as kindness. A second is *kalos*, which is much like *tov* in the Old Testament. It refers to something that is intrinsically good, fair, beautiful, or well adapted to circumstances. First Timothy 4:4 uses this word to talk about creation itself. The third is *agathosyne*. Paul uses this word more than the other New Testament writers, and it has a cosmic quality to it. While some people may be born with a natural *kalos*, *agathosyne* is a work of God, not of intrinsic human nature. If you have ever done anything powerfully good and courageous and later felt stunned that you did it, then you know what it feels like for the Spirit to do goodness through you.

A parishioner once told me a story of driving home from our inner-city church one evening after Bible study. As she drove through the darkened city streets among shadows and alleyways, she prayed that she would get home safely. While her nervousness was more conditioned than fact-based, it was no less real in her emotions. Suddenly, she saw a woman lying on the side of the road, struggling to rise. She heard the inner voice with which the Spirit often speaks say to her, "Stop." So she did.

She got out of the car to find a young woman in terrible distress. She had been raped and left in the woods far from where she lived. She had crawled and stumbled toward home until she could not anymore. My parishioner got her in her car. She asked the young woman if she wanted to go to the hospital. "No." She asked if she wanted to go to the police station. "No," she said. "I just want to go home.

Please take me home." In the course of that drive into, and through, some truly devastated neighborhoods, the young woman sat and wept most of the way. Through her weeping, her story unfolded, bit by bit. She had five children and few resources. Her husband had left her, though not before giving her HIV. (This was years before effective treatments.) She had just been raped and left in the woods. In the midst of her sobs, she asked my friend, "Do you think it is really possible for someone to turn their life around?" My friend said, "Yes, Stephanie. It is starting right now."

That story is an example of Spirit goodness leading a privileged woman through her fear, not just to take a battered young woman home, but to speak the truth of God to her with clarity and purpose. My parishioner befriended Stephanie and remained by her side for the rest of her life. Stephanie did die from AIDS, but her life changed the night of that drive. She blossomed. She changed her view of herself, and that changed the remainder of her days and the lives of her children. Goodness is faith on its feet doing things that set other things in motion. It is being the hands and feet of the Good Spirit taking lives and the world forward.

It is obvious from even a cursory reading of the Gospels that Jesus fully embodied the fruit of goodness/generosity. Gentle Jesus, meek and mild, is not entirely absent in the Gospels, but gentle Jesus is more like a condiment than the main dish.

In Luke 19:45, Jesus has just entered Jerusalem on an unbroken colt. There are no palm branches in this version of the story. There is just a band of people so longing for their lives to manifestly change that they sing psalms and throw down their cloaks, which represented the most valuable thing they owned. It was the one thing that could not be taken from them to pay a debt. Meanwhile, on the other side of town, Pilate, with all his warhorses and chariots with wheels of gold polished to catch the sun and blind the enemy, enters with his entourage to try to keep the peace during Passover. Spirit goodness on the one hand, the power of the state on the other. Jesus is unbowed by either the adulation showered upon him or the force gathering to keep him in line. He sees it all and weeps over the city and its inhabitants. Then he goes to the temple and creates some "good trouble."

When he arrives, he sees the marketing of faith for profit. He sees the exploitation of the faithful by the greedy and those who hold authority. He will have none of it. He turns over their tables, tramples their merchandise, and, in John's account (John 2:13–16), chases them out with a whip. Spirit goodness does not simply bewail oppression and exploitation. It does what it can, brings its energy to bear, to disrupt injustice whenever, wherever, and despite whatever.

Jesus' goodness often emerges from compassion and grief over the plight and the blindness of people. Jesus wept over Jerusalem, and those tears made him strong and ready to trouble the waters of exploitation and expediency. Jesus' goodness confounded norms and was met with controversy. We can expect the same in our day when the Spirit ripens goodness in our lives. Sometimes struggle is the fertilizer for maturity. Goodness does not sit down and say please and thank you to the oppressor for the crumbs that fall from the table. Jesus himself learned this from a Syrophoenician woman whom he initially dismissed (see Mark 7:24–30). Goodness includes resistance to power that erases the voices of those who bother or frighten those in power.

In the luncheon with Archbishop Desmond Tutu that I mentioned in chapter 4, I was awed by this man who was one of the great powers in the dismantling of apartheid in South Africa. A seedling at best in every aspect of the fruit of the Spirit myself, I at least had wisdom enough to recognize greatness when I saw it. I was seated across the narrow table from him. At one point he looked intently at me and said, "Pastor, tell me of your struggle." I was breathless with overwhelm. I have no memory of what hash of words stumbled out of me in answer. Mercifully. Maybe I said something about growing up in the Jim Crow South. Maybe I said something about trying to raise money for our shelter for homeless women and children. I do not remember. But what I do remember is how intently he focused on me and said, when I was spent, "There is braveness in you. You will need it."

I felt neither brave nor good that day. What I have since learned, however, is that courage is essential to goodness. Goodness will not take us where we want to go, as Jesus tells Peter in John 21:17–19. If we heed Jesus' call to feed his sheep, we will often be led by others to hard places and find that we have little choice in the matter. Goodness, faith on its feet, will take us where the love of God for the world needs us to go.

The clearest example of goodness taking the difficult but needed path is, of course, the crucifixion of Jesus. The Gospel writers see the no-turning-back point in Jesus' mission in different incidents. In Matthew, after Jesus' blistering rebuke of hypocrisy (23:1–36), it seems that the anointing of Jesus by the unnamed woman is Judas's breaking point (26:6–16). He just can't take it anymore—the scandal, the waste, the danger, the dashed expectations. In Luke, Satan instigates the betrayal (22:3).

Most moving to me, though, is John's account. There, in chapter 11, it is clearly love that sets the passion story in motion. Jesus knows that if he goes back to Jerusalem, he will not come out alive. He hears of the death of his friend Lazarus and how much his friends Mary and Martha need him. He hesitates for reasons of his own. But he goes. And what does he do? He weeps and agonizes at his friend's grave.

Then, as he always finds a way to do, he calls life out of that which seemed dead and without hope. From that moment, the cross was inevitable. The ground shifted under the feet of the universe after that, and the powerful always hate earthquakes, especially earthquakes that challenge their assumptions and control.

Compassion for the struggles and grief of people moves Jesus to generous goodness, to putting it all on the line. Sometimes it does that for us as well. Could it be that struggle, like no-pain, no-gain exercise programs, makes the muscle of goodness strong? Could it be that compassionate tears water the Spirit's shoots of goodness? I believe so. In any case, goodness will not be free from sorrow on occasion or from danger.

In the New Testament letters, the authors talk about goodness as everything from a prerequisite for teaching (Rom. 15:14) to "fruit of the light," or enlightenment (Eph. 5:9). What is clear is that goodness is a way of talking about how God acts for, with, and through believers. In Luke 18:19, Jesus tells the rich man who comes to him searching for a way to quiet his spiritual restlessness that only God is good. That being the case, the goodness we do is God doing it through us.

WEEDS IN THE
GARDEN OF GOODNESS

Hate can strangle out the shoots of each aspect of the Spirit's fruit. Goodness is no exception. We cannot be good and wish another harm, even the harm of staying in the place we have decided to put them. We cannot mature in goodness if we choose thoughts or behaviors that tear another down or block them from the life of dignity for which they were created. In the beautiful rendering of God's values that we call the Ten Commandments, hateful and demeaning actions are considered violations of the mandate not to steal or to kill. We can do both with words, actions, and policies without shedding a drop of blood.

To clear the weeds for goodness, we have to examine our own prejudices. We have to ask ourselves whom we secretly despise and think of as "less than." We have to look at the large and small demeaning actions we take and those we fail to confront. Awareness itself can be a powerful weed killer when it arises in a spirit of prayer, humility, and willingness to change.

Hypocrisy is a stubborn weed in the garden of goodness. The root for the word "hypocrisy" refers to actors on a stage, people who pretend to be someone they are not in order to entertain or gain favor from others. Gradually, it came to refer to people who live one way in public and another way in private. It also refers to those who expect certain behaviors from others that they do not expect from themselves. This tendency is particularly dangerous in the religious and political spheres. It can wear us out and confuse us when we try to keep on a mask in our personal relationships. It is exhausting to try to be what others want us to be or to live up to some image we have in our heads of the perfect mom, dad, spouse, employee.

When we choose to live hypocritically in our systems and institutions, the damage is truly devastating. We quickly lose the ability to identify the truth from the pageant. We can do "right things," but the motive is for gain of something—money, power, esteem, love. We can also do "wrong things" and convince ourselves that they are not wrong because they serve an end that we have decided is right. Perhaps this is the mind bend into which the scribes and Pharisees fell that led to Jesus' scathing rebuke of them (Matt. 23:1–36). They did what they did not for the common good but to receive honor or power.

Since goodness arises from a zeal for the truth, goodness and lies cannot occupy the same space at the same time, even if, for reasons of our own, we have accepted lies as truth. Spirit truth recognizes that lies inevitably destroy not only the one who propagates them but also those who fall into their web. The prophet Isaiah puts this beautifully when he denounces social injustice in 5:18–20: "Woe to those who drag iniquity along with cords of falsehood. . . . Woe to those who call evil good and good evil, who put darkness for light and light for darkness, who put bitter for sweet and sweet for bitter!" The prophet makes it clear that hypocrisy, when normalized in those with power, will always harm those who seek to expose it.

Lies and hypocrisy, or as we euphemistically call them sometimes, "alternative facts," imply that there is a different reality that we would prefer to inhabit, so we become our own little gods and create it for ourselves, worship it with our whole selves, and serve it with our lives if necessary. We quickly become false witnesses who cannot tell the difference between truth and lies and who will zealously defend as truth what is really a lie. Very little true and lasting goodness can break ground when we fall into that trap.

We have seen this throughout history. The scribes and Pharisees believed they were right in seeking Jesus' death. Judas probably did too, at least at first. Rome thought that public executions of Christians were right and necessary for the public good. The people of Salem thought it was right to burn witches. The advocates of slavery claimed to believe that it was for the good of the enslaved because they were not quite human and couldn't take care of themselves. The legacy of those choices and hundreds more lives on in different guises today as we continue to struggle to live up to our highest values for all citizens.

It takes courage and generosity of spirit to stand against the lies that strangle out true goodness. In recent days, we have seen election workers, jurists, prosecutors, whistle-blowers, elected officials, and police subject to personal attacks on themselves and their families. It would be easy and understandable for them to give up and ask someone else to take the heat for a while. Yet many do not. At risk to life and limb, they go to work every day to serve the public good. They choose *agathosyne* over the easy path. Mature goodness requires that we be the change we want to see and not the lies.

To confront hypocrisy, lies, and hate wherever we find them is a tough duty, but it is also incumbent on followers of Jesus. In Matthew 18:15, Jesus addresses this issue directly and gives instructions on how to reprove others who are doing harm. It is a process. It is utterly respectful. It is both personal and communal. It sometimes produces desired results, and sometimes does not. Its motivation is always to bring the other goodness, to encourage goodness in the other. It is not to punish but rather to restore. If nothing works, then for the sake of the community itself, ties are broken but prayers never cease.

The problem, of course, is that we are all fallible and that we see only what we are able to see at any given moment. We can be wrong in our assessments about almost anything. We can even convince ourselves that what we see or want is the sum total of what the Spirit sees and wants. In our daily lives, the desire for goodness to emerge in us can leave us with many unsettling questions. Like Pilate, we may wonder what is the truth for which we are to offer our zeal. What is the role of accommodation? Is it possible to be good and administer unjust laws? If there is a conflict between different-seeming "goods," how do we decide which is our priority? Because of this, true Spirit goodness in human beings is always marked by humility. We don't want to be right. We want to be of use to God and our neighbors.

THE FRAGRANCE OF GOODNESS

At heart, goodness is about how we choose to use our power. We all have some power, even when we don't know how to harness it. We are each different, and God has a will for us that includes goodness, manifesting itself in exactly the way that is best for us and for those around us. Sometimes that goodness will take us to the streets in protest against injustice. Sometimes it will take us to boardrooms or city council chambers to advocate for the common good in policies and procedures. Sometimes it will take us into the age-old confrontation of hate and prejudice. Sometimes the fight will take us into the murky realm of politics. Sometimes it will take us into the heart of the church itself. Sometimes it will lead us to courageous action that can change the world. Sometimes it will be active and confrontive. Sometimes it will be displayed in a breathless picture of pacifism. Sometimes it will be released in small and nuanced bursts of committed daily actions.

A few years ago, a friend told me a story about attending a glorious wedding in San Francisco when she was in college. The church was filled with flowers and packed with people. The couple had already been through some hard times and weathered them with a deepening love. They were best friends, and they were marrying. After the wedding, there was a beautiful reception with a band and a large, raised dance floor.

My friend was sitting at the table with some of her friends enjoying the food and drink. She and her friends were laughing and filled with warmth and joy when she noticed an older guest using a wheelchair. She watched him go around and around the edge of the dance floor, trying to get his chair up on the platform. He finally succeeded in getting onto the dance floor and began to sway in his chair to the music with his head lifted toward the fairy lights hanging above. As she watched him, she felt compelled to go to him. She introduced herself and asked him to dance. His eyes filled with tears and he said, "When I was a young man, I was a professional dancer. There was an accident, and I was paralyzed from the waist down. My dance partner was killed." He said, "It was the greatest grief of my life. When I danced with my partner, who I loved so dearly, I could feel God's pleasure. I could tip my face up, and I was filled with the joy of the Lord. It was like heaven opened and poured goodness into my whole body and soul."

My friend said to him, "I would love to be your dance partner this evening." She took his hands, and they danced, he in his chair, she in her party shoes. They danced until the band stopped playing. As they parted, he looked at her and said, "You have done me a great kindness." As she walked back to the table with her friends, she said she had never felt God's presence and goodness so completely before.

This story could just as easily be an illustration of kindness or even love. The aspects of the fruit of the Spirit are so intertwined that they cannot, and need not, be pulled apart. Still, I think this story illustrates goodness or generosity because of the very physicality of it. The young woman got up from her table where she was enjoying a carefree time with her friends because she felt compelled to come to the aid of someone who could not easily overcome the obstacles before him and who was in obvious pain. She saw struggle and reacted to alleviate it. In so doing, both were elevated together. Goodness is not always about doing the big things. It is about using our power actively for the good of others.

As Spirit goodness begins to ripen in us, we find that the Spirit desires that we treat ourselves with active generous goodness as well. If we think of goodness as faith on its feet, actively seeking justice and well-being while zealously seeking after the truth, we learn that it requires a clear-eyed view of ourselves and our own needs in order for it to mature.

Expressing goodness to ourselves is not as simple as exercising willpower, although that may be needed. Goodness toward the self requires that we have the courage to look at ourselves without the masks and delusions we often think of as normal.

Once a parishioner thought I was looking a little worn-out. She worked at a fancy spa and gave me a free spa day with massages and facials, new makeup . . . the works. It was wonderful. At the end of the day I was even allowed to choose a new outfit from the spa store. I remember trying on dresses with my perfectly done hair and makeup and thinking that I really looked marvelous. When I got home and looked at myself in my own mirror, I looked nothing like the image I had seen in the spa mirror. I later asked my friend what was up with that. She said, "Oh, that is a marketing mirror. It shows us as we wish we were — or how we could be, with a little extra help."

Many of us live with our gaze firmly planted in the marketing mirror. We use our homes, spouses, children, accomplishments, and aspirations to shore up an image of ourselves that is, at best, seen through a mirror dimly, as Paul puts it in 1 Corinthians 13. We often know that our lived reality does not live up to the image we espouse, but we are in love with that image, think it is the way things should be, and so we worship it as some kind of idol. If we do that long enough, somewhere along the way we lose touch with what is really true about our deepest selves. When that happens, it not only distorts our self-image but also makes it hard for us to see ourselves and circumstances as good enough. Self-delusion and self-goodness are never happy bedfellows.

Sometimes we take on the images others have of us and come to believe them too. This creates internal oppression that has deep roots that are hard to pull. Once I received a call to serve as pastor of a church in an area where I had always wanted to live. It seemed like a good fit for me. I was excited about the possibility. I was excited, that is, until the pastoral nominating committee chairperson called to talk with me about terms. He said, "We hope you will be happy here, Eugenia. The committee wants you to know that we were not unanimous in offering you this call, but you are a woman and so we can afford you."

Mercifully, I was aware enough to hear the sirens and see the flashing warning lights on that one and did not accept the call. But for years afterward I never confronted the fact that I was consistently one of the lowest-paid pastors in my presbytery. "I'm lucky to have work," I told myself. "You are lucky to have work," others told me. It was years before I had the maturity to advocate with *agathosyne* for myself. Even then, I was sometimes called uppity or selfish. Doing good toward yourself, just as surely as doing good for others, has consequences. It is just necessary for our own healing and wholeness.

CONCLUSION

As goodness ripens, we sometimes need to make "good trouble" for ourselves in concrete ways. We need to disrupt patterns that are doing us harm. We need to get in the way of expectations that are killing us or policies that are limiting our full expression. We need to learn to stand up for ourselves in harmful situations, whether those are toxic relationships or toxic structures or habits.

It is often hard in tough or hidebound circumstances to do *agathosyne* at all. There are some signposts to remember, though. To mature, goodness requires loving motives. Goodness corrects but never humiliates. We can't do this kind of good for others while hating and wanting to defeat them. Nor can we do it when we are not offering goodness to ourselves.

Goodness always contains a kind of submission that requires that we release our mental place as the center of our own lives and allow that place to rightly be occupied by God. As we learn the disciplines of recognizing and weeding out the obstacles to goodness, a subtle shift takes place in the soul.

We can start by acknowledging our common humanity and frailties. We can ask God to make us gentle toward others' faults as we ask God to be gentle toward them as well. *Agathosyne* has an easier time growing in us when we are praying for our enemies as well as our friends and when we are immersed in the mystery for which Jesus prays to the Father in John 17:21: that they may all be one.

As James Baldwin said on many occasions, "Not everything that is faced can be changed; but nothing can be changed until it is faced."[10] Goodness, as all the aspects of the fruit do, requires that we do a fair bit of self-examination and weed pulling in order to create a fertile environment for growth and good change. Delusions will strangle out goodness, as will hate, unforgiveness, and cowardice. *Agathosyne* is active, zealous, committed, energetic faith that moves out on behalf of the truth of God's love and values in the lives of people, systems, and the planet. The good we do may be to create something new, or it may be to disrupt something old and worn. The motive is not mere success. The motive is to continue the work of Jesus in our own lives, with our whole heart, soul, and body. *Agathosyne* is the ever-generous offering of our lives to be used by God for the furthering of God's realm on earth as in heaven.

As we learn the disciplines of recognizing and weeding out the obstacles to goodness we find that we no longer waste our energy by grasping and conserving. Rather, we spend our energy generously, placing all that we are and have in service to God, others, and our moment in history. We come to understand deeply that the way to fix what is wrong is to do what is right.

A WEEK FOR TENDING GENEROUS GOODNESS

Day One: "I myself feel confident about you, my brothers and sisters, that you yourselves are full of goodness, filled with all knowledge, and able to instruct one another" (Rom. 15:14). Paul often uses the word *agathosyne* to mean acting in an honorable way that gives freely of the self (there's that connection to generosity). Here, Paul tells us that the ability to give of oneself lavishly is tied to our personal knowledge of Christ coupled with our willingness to help one another to learn. In what ways do you give lavishly of yourself to others? Do you find that you sometimes give too much or too little? How do you think that affects goodness maturing in you? How does your knowledge of Christ help you find just the right balance? Notice today how internally generous you feel with your time, your influence, your resources, and your power. Ask God throughout the day to enable you to be "full of goodness."

Day Two: "Let love be genuine; hate what is evil; hold fast to what is good" (Rom. 12:9). Sometimes it seems easier to hold on to the bad things in life than the good. Earthquakes, wars, poverty, and division fill the news and can leave us feeling infected with the negative. Paul tells us that our love cannot be a hypocritical yes-but kind of thing. Rather, each day we are to cling to the good, even in our opponents, as to a rope thrown to a person gone overboard. What are the truly good things in your life and in our world? Today make a list of at least ten Spirit goodness things. Print the list and put it in your wallet or on your phone. When you take out your wallet to pay for something or pick up your phone to check messages, read over the list. When you feel tempted to focus on the harsh and the negative, add to your list of goodness instead. You will soon feel new energy to notice goodness and allow the Spirit to mature goodness in your life and actions. Today, thank God for every good gift.

Day Three: "The fruit of the light is found in all that is good and right and true" (Eph. 5:9). The author of Ephesians is trying to get his friends to realize that not everyone who claims to have the truth actually does have it. Their church is being torn apart by false teachers who are telling them that they have it all wrong. Here we are reminded that when the light of Christ truly shines in our hearts and lives, it will be displayed in our actions as truth, holiness, and goodness. How does the light of Christ shine most brightly in you? How does that light illumine your actions and draw you to do good things in your daily life? Take a moment sometime today to light a candle and gaze at the flame. Remember that Christ is the light to your path. In the presence of that little light, ask God how you might shine with goodness today. Listen for Spirit intuitions and nudges for answers. Look for one small thing that you do today to make a difference for the good in the life of another.

Day Four: "To this end we always pray for you, asking that our God will make you worthy of his call and will fulfill by his power every good resolve and work of faith" (2 Thess. 1:11). Our attempts to live with the fruit of goodness flowing through us are not solely up to our willpower, determination, or awareness. The Spirit is constantly at work in us, making us better than we have ever been before. What are some of the areas in which you think you have grown morally finer? Do you find that you speak up more in the face of injustice? Do you find that you are more willing to go out of your way to help those who have challenges? Think of all the expressions of goodness that you admire in others. Do you see any of those qualities beginning to emerge in your life too? Notice where you have grown and where you need to tend the soil better. Ask God to work a good character into you and to start today.

Day Five: In your own Bible, read Matthew 26:6–13. This is the story of a repentant woman who anoints Jesus with some very expensive ointment. The disciples are aghast. They see her action as both shockingly unseemly and financially irresponsible. Jesus sees things differently. Jesus quiets his friends by saying she has done a good thing for him. Spirit goodness always results in radical generosity that flows without hesitation from a transformed heart and worldview. In what ways has pondering generous goodness opened your heart or worldview? What fears or certainties hold you back from true goodness? On what, and on whom, do you lavish your generous goodness? Who gets little or nothing but leftovers? Ask the Spirit today to bring to your awareness moments when you are generous with goodness and moments when you refuse.

Day Six: In your own Bible, read Matthew 21:12–13. This is the story we considered earlier in this chapter of Jesus running the vendors and money changers out of the temple. Sometimes moral goodness requires "tough love." To do a good thing in a bad situation is rarely popular and often misunderstood. Yet as Christians, we cannot consider ourselves morally good if we allow injustice, exploitation, and casual immorality to reign without a word of protest. Protest from love and for love is an important tool of goodness. Mature Spirit goodness is never passive or abstract. It is active and concrete. How might you speak up for justice, fairness, equity, and truth today? Is anyone being bullied, shunned, or rejected in your workplace, your neighborhood, your child's school? How might you do something good in those circumstances? Are there things in your family toward which you have turned a blind eye for too long? Who are the people you think of as "them"? What might you really have in common? What might Jesus need to run out of your heart today?

Questions for Reflection and Discussion

1. Think about the questions asked in Day Six of this week's daily practice. Brainstorm with your group how you might choose actions of goodness.

2. How do you think the concepts of goodness and generosity each help to define *agathosyne*?

3. What do you think of the concept of good trouble? In your community or church, are there any habits or policies that you think Jesus would choose to get in the way of?

   [handwritten note in margin: Comfort the trouble + trouble the comfortable]

4. Of all the weeds in goodness's garden, which do you find most troublesome? Have you found ways to deal with them in your life? Share with others what has worked for you.

5. Can you think of a story to share about someone showing goodness or generosity to you?

6. Did anything in this chapter surprise you? If so, share that with your group.

CHAPTER 8

TENDING THE
SHOOTS OF FAITHFULNESS

*Faith is taking the first step even when you
don't see the whole staircase.*
—Martin Luther King Jr.

When I was a pastor in the Denver metro area, I
lived in a beautiful apartment with a Colorado blue
spruce outside my living room window. Nothing gave me
a cozier feeling than sitting in my comfy chair with a cup
of coffee and watching the snow fall and weigh down the
sturdy branches. I did not have a mountain view, but my
patio opened onto a beautiful meadow. Sometimes it was
filled with wildflowers, sometimes with deer and antelope
tracks in the snow. Sometimes just summer grasses. The
winters in Denver, though, were a shock to me.

One year it was snowing on Memorial Day, and I
decided that summer would finally come if I primed the
pump a bit. So I went to buy a barbecue grill. I donned
boots and gloves, got in my car, and headed across town to
a mall that had advertised a sale.

At a spot near the mall where two multilane freeways meet, traffic lurched to a stop. I had no idea what was going on until I saw a beautiful young dog running around the traffic, trailing a pink leash. People were trying to catch her to no avail. I opened my door to lend a hand, and the little thing jumped in my car and crouched on the floorboard on the passenger side. People got back in their cars, but nobody came to look for the dog.

She was bleeding. I thought she had been hit, so I took her to my vet. As it turned out, she had not been hit by a car; she had been beaten with a chain until she was bloody. The vet tracked down the owner, who said that they were disciplining her and she pulled away. They did not want her anymore. That is how my first keeshond, Keesie, entered my life.

She was sweet but terrified from the start. I already had a small terrier, Megan, who basically rolled her eyes but did not complain. For days, Keesie sat trembling under the dining room table. She would eat only out of my hand, although she didn't resist going out on a leash. One night I was sitting in my big chair with little Megan beside me when I saw Keesie get up and sit back down several times, as if she were trying to gather her courage. Suddenly, she sprang from under the table and leapt into my lap. That night was a turning point.

A month or two later she had progressed to the point that sometimes I let her off leash to run in the meadow. She loved it. One day I came home from church on my lunch hour to walk the dogs. Keesie ran like the wind in the meadow that day. I was afraid she would go too far, so I called her. She seemed to pivot in midair to run back to me. She sat down beside me, took the hem of my skirt in her mouth, and looked up in adoration while she waited for further instructions. I thought in that moment that I was witnessing exactly what the Bible talks about as faith or faithfulness. Faithfulness is not so much about what we choose to believe in our minds as it is about whom we choose to trust.

FAITHFULNESS IN THE BIBLE

In the Old Testament, the word most often translated as faithfulness, *'emunah,* means to be certain of something or someone. God's people learn what faithfulness is by observing how God behaves. God is both faithful *and* trustworthy. Those qualities are two sides of one coin. It is impossible for God *not* to be faithful and trustworthy. These qualities call us to reciprocate. Because we rely on God's faithfulness and trustworthiness, we return faithfulness and trustworthiness to God and to others on behalf of God.

The sturdy certainty that God can be trusted is what allows Abraham to gather his belongings and leave his home to find the land of promise with no road map at all. It is his deep certainty that God is trustworthy that allows him, years later, to agree to return to God the beloved child of promise, Isaac. Abraham trusted that God had a bigger and finer plan for him and his son. So he put his foot to the path, unsure of what would happen next, but confident that both he and his son were safe when acting faithfully.

Did Abraham know that God would provide an alternative path in his tough journey? There are hints in the text that he believed that. Still, he acted on his one deep certainty: God was faithful and trustworthy. Abraham had developed the capacity, through his ups and downs, the joys, the setbacks, the personal failures, the painful losses, to trust that God's way was the only way. So he stepped out. Like Keesie observing me and Megan from beneath the dining table, Abraham observed God's faithfulness and decided to take the risk of trusting it.

The breakdown of trust between God and God's people in the Hebrew Scriptures leads to profound devastations for individuals and communities. In Hosea, the prophet talks about the rupture in Israel's national and religious life being like a faithless wife who panders after other loves. Patterned on his own marital woes, Hosea sees God's people's unfaithfulness, and it leaves the prophet, and God, grief stricken and wondering why God's love was not enough. He knows that hope can be durable only when faithfulness is an observable characteristic of God's people.

There are consequences when God's people are unfaithful and flee from God. Even then, God is faithful. The Presbyterian Church (U.S.A.)'s Brief Statement of Faith puts it this way:

> In everlasting love,
>> the God of Abraham and Sarah chose a covenant people
>> to bless all families of the earth.
>
> Hearing their cry,
>> God delivered the children of Israel
>> from the house of bondage.
>
> Loving us still,
>> God makes us heirs with Christ of the covenant.
>
> Like a mother who will not forsake her nursing child,
>> like a father who runs to welcome the prodigal home,
>> God is faithful still.[11]

The tending work of faithfulness is to build confidence that God is trustworthy and then to become trustworthy to God in return.

Once when I was fairly new to a parish, I was working on a sermon on Abraham's offering of Isaac back to God.

Sometimes in the afternoons I took time in the beautiful Gothic sanctuary to sit and feel the prayers of the centuries. The beauty of the stained glass windows always soothed and awakened my soul if I was feeling tired or fearful. That particular day, I was feeling tired but more hopeful than fearful. I was walking in and out among the pews praying for the people that I confidently believed God was about to bring to our church when I felt the Spirit's inner voice say, "Give me that."

I was thunderstruck and sank onto one of the pews. "What?" I said. "All of that," the Spirit seemed to reply. "Your hopes, your dreams, your loves, and your desires." Before I could even think, I said aloud, "No!" I was immediately ashamed.

Then a picture came to my mind of my beloved father, the rock of my life, standing on our front porch waving to me, as he always did, as I drove away. At that point, he was beginning to wrestle with Parkinson's disease. I was very concerned about him. I felt the Spirit say, "Give him to me." And unlike Abraham, my faith was not strong enough in that instant. I could not offer my dreams and my father wholeheartedly to God. Something inside me constricted. That moment passed quickly. As I got up to head back to my office, I felt the Spirit again nudge me, "Do you trust me? We have work to do on that."

There was a lot involved in that sacred moment where my lack of faith was laid bare to me. There was no small amount of ego and desire to be the miracle worker in the church and in my family. This was, of course, no surprise to God. Even so, there was tender clarity and compassion in that encounter. I did not feel chastised. I felt accompanied, and I knew that I was entering into a season in which the Spirit desired to bring trust to greater maturity in my life. I knew with certainty what I believed about God and about the life of faith, but trust and relinquishing my life to my trustworthy God were not yet strong. I could, like Abraham, put my foot to the path, but unlike Abraham, I was always looking for a way to control the outcome. The seed was there, but tending was needed.

In the New Testament, the Greek word translated as faith or faithfulness is *pistis* in one of its forms. Occasionally, the word is used to mean the content of our belief, as in a statement of faith. (See Phil. 1:27 and Gal. 1:23 and 3:23 as examples.) Most often by far, however, the word describes a deeply settled trust, especially in God, Christ, or the spiritual life into which we are called. This trust remains steadfast in all circumstances. In Paul's later letters, we can see how the years and their trials have deepened his trust. In passage after passage (such as Rom. 3:25; 1 Cor. 2:5; 15:14; and 1 Thess. 3:2), we learn that as discipleship deepens, faith is more about trust in God than doctrinal purity. Why? Because faith is relational at its core, and evidence of it can be seen not just in acceptance of basic tenets, but, even more so, in a settled disposition toward life, God, and a future that is marked by courageous loving actions on behalf of others.

Pistis does not rest on, or result from, proof. It is neither proved nor disproved by what happens in our lives or in our world. As the thirteenth-century theologian Thomas Aquinas put it, "To one who has faith, no explanation is necessary. To one without, no explanation is possible."[12]

Pistis rests squarely on who God is. Over time, as it deepens, it becomes the kind of assurance spoken of in Hebrews 11:1: "Now faith is the assurance of things hoped for, the conviction of things not seen." Faith as mature fruit produces a calm delight that holds us up in travail. It also results in powerful love-struck actions that we feel compelled to take.

In Scripture, God's faithfulness toward us is lavish and undaunted even by the cross. It challenges us to respond in kind. It is a gift of the Spirit. It may sometimes feel weak in us, but it is in reality the sturdiest of things because it does not rest on either our understanding or our habits. It rises and does its work in us when we are aware and when we are unaware. We may reject a set of beliefs. We may run from the idea of a trustworthy personal God. We may—out of pain, or history, or an overly literal interpretation of Scripture—decide that God is unworthy of our trust or worship. We may decide God does not exist and put our trust in other things entirely. Those choices will certainly have consequences. What they will not do, however, is make God untrustworthy or stop God's faithfulness to us. The seed of faith is within each of us. It will find its way to the light one way or another.

I once had a wonderful, feisty parishioner who struggled all his life with his faith. He was a wealthy businessman and really didn't want much in the way of ethics to shape his choices. When I talked with him about the welfare of his workers or the importance of supporting justice ministries, he listened and basically patted me on the head. He had been raised in the church, been baptized in the church, and as a younger man served on the council of the church. But as he got older and more powerful, he was beset with doubts and a sterling apathy toward all things of faith. Even when he became terminally ill, he wasn't sure if the whole thing was "just bunk."

We talked a lot in his last year. I could see that as his body struggled, his soul was struggling too. "How can you be so sure, Eugenia?" he said to me one day while I was sitting by his bed and, at his request, reading the Psalms to him. I'm sure I said something inane. We can't take the faith journey for each other, after all.

A few days later, he slipped into a coma. The family asked me to come when it seemed the end was near. So, again, I sat by him reading the Psalms with the family and the hospice nurse standing by his bed. Suddenly, he opened his eyes and seemed to look at someone standing elevated at the foot of the bed. "I'll be damned," he said. "It really is true. It was you all along." He shined. Every part of his body relaxed. His smile was electric. Within minutes, he died.

The fruit of faithfulness reminds us that God will chase us down in the streets of our lives. Faithful God will wait and watch and touch us when we know and when we don't. God will never give up, never refuse to be faithful and trustworthy to the end and beyond. That characteristic of God is within us, too, and we, like God, can put it to work. It may take some soul clearing to do it.

WEEDS IN THE GARDEN OF FAITH

One of the powerful weeds that can steal nutrients from faith is a skewed sense of self. That can be either an elevated sense of our own power and capacities or a distorted and too-limited one. If it is too elevated, we can lose the sense that we need God at all. If we have too low a sense of self, we can come to believe that even God is not powerful enough to put us back together again. Both of those poles are built on lies. None of us is all that our press agents declare, and none of us is as little as we sometimes believe. Weeding out the damaging lies we carry about ourselves is demanding work that requires tender and timely attention.

Just last week a friend made a casual remark that hurt my feelings deeply. My initial response was to drop a wall between us and run away to lick my wound. The weed of needing to be thought wonderful at all times was wrapped tightly around my heart. I felt crushed by it. I also knew that I needed some time and space to reflect on what happened. So I began to ask myself some questions. Did he want to hurt me? Was I responding to what he said or what I feared that he meant? If he did mean it, did that mean that he no longer cared about or valued me? Was he saying I was a failure? Did his remark offer me information that I should think about? Was there something I needed to change? Was he hurting in some way, and I got in the way of that hurt? Could I trust him in the future?

As I thought and prayed through those questions and thought about our long friendship, the weed of needing to be super special at all times began to loosen. My attention allowed the Spirit to clear some pesky weeds that were causing me pain and had the capacity to derail our friendship. A few days later my friend and I had a great conversation in which we both learned something about each other that restored our trust. Until I did that inner-weeding work, however, I was trusting wrong things and missing the big ones. As Jesus said to the Pharisees in his scathing rebuke of their tithing mint and cumin while ignoring the weighty aspects of justice and faith (Matt. 23:23), I was allowing something small to take up my energy and blind me to bigger things that were more important.

One way to identify weeds that strangle faithfulness and trust is to listen to what you say to yourself when faced with challenging experiences. Are you responding from an inner script that is telling you that you are not able or lovable? Are you responding from the belief that others are wrong, wicked, unlovable, dangerous? When we are uprooting the weeds of sad stories we tell about ourselves, it helps to do so with kindness and joyful expectation of new growth. Remember that the weeds are not our enemies. They are guides.

Another powerful weed in faithfulness's garden is ego-blinded self-reliance. Many of us were raised to be independent, self-sufficient, and, insofar as possible, in control. Perhaps as children, if there was a crisis in the family, we were given more responsibility than we were ready for and came to believe that the whole house of cards would fall if we did not keep it upright. As adults, we may have come to believe that we were our own little gods and applied that subconscious belief to our relationships and our faith.

Maybe we naturally excelled in our youth and came to believe that our awards defined us. At times like that we can come to think that faith is weakness, a crutch, a sign of our own vulnerability, and so faithfulness is needless or dangerous. When we find ourselves in that attitude, we often have made our power, privilege, accolades into little gods, and our true faithfulness to God and neighbor gets lost in those competing voices.

The opposite is often true as well. Maybe we were let down so often by others that we became unable to rely on others—much less on God. In either excessive self-reliance or fear-based distrust, we may not be able to rely on God deeply because we have somehow been lost, and with that wound, we lost our felt capacity to trust and be trusting.

LOSING AND HEALING A LOST SELF

We begin to lose our true selves, the ones who are capable of mature, clear-eyed faith, with our first trauma. Often we don't even remember that event or the self we left behind in order to deal with it. It doesn't matter if it was big or small. It just had to be something that shook our security and that we felt we had to manage or control when we could not.

When I was five, I had my first life-threatening illness. I already had lung issues by then, but that year I developed a devastating case of double pneumonia and was put in the hospital under an oxygen tent, with cutdowns in my little ankles because my other veins had collapsed from the IVs. I remember how the tent distorted my vision. I remember the isolation of it. To cope I took little snub-nosed scissors and soft pastel paper and made paper chains to decorate the inside of the tent. Each time I made a chain, the nurses tore it down. My attempt to cope was thwarted, and I didn't know how to process that. Was I bad to make the chains? Was that why I was sick?

Later in school, when children were bored, a classmate poked fun at my severe allergies, saying, "Let's get a cat and watch Genie blow up." Little by little, I shrank inside. If I had had the vocabulary at that age, I would have labeled myself defective. To compensate for that, I had to excel. I had to be a miracle. "Just Genie" disappeared for decades. Because of that I clung to control so hard that my faith, while unwavering, was not the enormous relief and release that it is intended to be.

The Bible calls us to the faith of a little child. That is not just a generic image of openness, trust, and powerlessness. It is also a call to return to the child we once were before human experience took us away from that unique self. Our wounds are detours sometimes, but they can also lead us to unexpected gifts. We cannot, however, allow them to become our excuses. Faith is not naturally weak. It is naturally strong. It is just trampled on occasionally.

Faith is more resilient at some times than others. To be resilient, we need to learn to distinguish between our essential child nature that loves, sees, trusts, and grows, on the one hand, and that remains infantile, refuses responsibility, and screams our heads off when things don't suit us, on the other. When we can tell the difference between those two things, faith becomes a childlike experience of joyful safety that arises from an honest understanding of ourselves. We can lean into it with confidence no matter what is happening around us.

OBSTACLES TO GROWING IN FAITH

Faith can be stunted by too much fear, grief, violence, and unexamined prejudice. Sometimes those things come together with terrible results. Consider the April 2023 shooting in Kansas City of Ralph Yarl, an exceptional young student whose mom asked him to pick up his younger siblings from a friend's house. He went to the wrong street. When Yarl rang the doorbell, the resident saw only a sixteen-year-old Black boy on his porch, not a lost youth. He shot him in the head and, while the teen was bleeding on the porch, shot him again. The teen ran to three houses before he found someone willing to help him.

This is both shocking and unsurprising in contemporary American culture. Was the shooter genuinely afraid? If so, why? Was he angry that his neighborhood was slowly integrating? Did he distrust all Black people? Had he had experiences that fueled his "stand your ground" ethic? Who knows. Maybe all of that. Maybe something else. What is clear, though, is that when prejudice, fear, and pain conspire, they can rob us of the ability to see the full humanity of others, and of ourselves. The writer of 1 John 4:12 reminds us that God's love is perfected in us as we open our hearts in active love to others. We cannot rely on God—that is, act in faithfulness—when we despise and fear God's children and decide we are justified in taking their lives in our own hands.

It can be hard to mature in faith when our personal lives are fraught with chaos, danger, and fear. Trusting God in the midst of the storms of life requires making a choice and, sometimes, overriding our emotions of fear, grief, and guilt with the powerful love of our faithful God.

When Jesus' disciples encountered a fierce storm at sea (Matt. 8:23–27), Jesus was in the boat with his friends, sound asleep. His reliance on the Father was so deep and certain, he would have slept in peace through the whole thing if his friends had not panicked. In the face of their fear, he woke up and spoke the storm into calm. How could he do that? From Matthew's point of view, he did it because his faith never wavered while the disciples' faith seems to have jumped overboard. In the calming of the storm, Jesus reminds us that even when we are terrified, there is nothing ultimate to fear. What can a mere storm do to us if even death has no power? What can the waters of chaos and fear do to us when our lives are eternally tucked into God?

We may also struggle to trust when our expectations are thwarted. Then, we can find it difficult to celebrate God's presence and trust the new thing that is happening. If a pandemic comes and we have to learn new ways of being church, either we can trust what God may yet do and in so doing thrive, or we can become stuck and find ourselves losing our trust altogether. If we have to reassess how we interact with others for their safety, we can come to see those around us as burdens rather than siblings and write them off rather than seeking God's ever-creative ways forward. If others disagree with us, we may disengage or become mean, stunting our ability to act faithfully. Faithfulness is a gift and also a muscle that we exercise by daily choosing to trust.

One of the greatest obstacles to maturing faith is graceless theology. If we have been taught that we are never good enough, always a disappointment, and that God is in a perpetual fury looking for ways to punish us into compliance, it can be hard to trust God at all. If our faith was largely nurtured on the threat of hell, and not the compassion of a father welcoming the prodigal and a risen Savior cooking fish on the beach for his bumfuzzled, betraying disciples, then it can be very hard for faith to ripen. If we have been beaten with narrow interpretations of sacred Scripture to the point that we think it is impossible to win God's favor and that we are despised, then, if faith survives at all, it will be based on fear and not love. That will never hold us up when times are hard. Faith arises from God's goodness and compassion. Faithfulness ripens on ever-expanding grace. This, of course, does not mean that sin is inconsequential. It is deeply consequential. It is just remedied. And it is remedied by grace alone.

UNEXPECTED ANGELS

Our soul garden may be full of weeds. We may have to gird up our loins and do some painful pulling. We may have to do that frequently and go over the same patch many times. Even so, the Spirit sends us amazing graces to help us do the hard work and to remind us of the wonders that come from trusting that God is with, within, and among us.

One Maundy Thursday a small group of the faithful gathered in my inner-city church to worship on that holy night. The gorgeous stained glass windows were dark. The sanctuary had a somber feel, befitting the night. Our associate pastor had baked bread for Communion. The from-the-oven smell mixed with the heady scent of dark wine and moved through the small crowd like the breath of angels.

At one point, a stranger entered the sanctuary. He was bedraggled and weaving a bit as he stumbled down the aisle to sit near the front with the small congregation. His coat was threadbare, and he held his worn hat in his hands. He probably lived on the streets somewhere near the church. Most of us thought he had come in to get warm. We went on with the service. We quietly remembered a last Passover meal, the disciples sleeping while Jesus prayed, his betrayal with a kiss.

When the time came to receive the sacrament, the man came forward with the other parishioners. When he got to where I was holding the glorious loaf of bread, he took a sizable chunk and lifted it to his mouth reverently. In a surprising baritone voice he said, "This is so good! Oh my! This is so, so good. May I have some more?" I told him that after everyone had had a bit he could have the rest. After all were served, I handed him the loaf.

Throughout the rest of the service, the man sat humming, munching, and saying, "MMMMM! MMMM!" It was like a prayer. It was like a hymn. There was not a dry eye in the place. The windows dark, the candles flickering, the spring storms brewing, we sat there together. The people of privilege who wound their way downtown at night, the women who lived in the shelter in our basement, the clergy who could hardly breathe from the poignancy of it, we sat there together in the mystery and the wonder of that sacred night and that mighty sacrament.

We never saw that man again. Someone bought him a hotel room for the night, gave him a referral to the men's shelter and a few bucks for food, but he never wandered into our church again. In a very real way, though, he never left. He was forever a part of us. For those present on that one holy night, every time thereafter that we approached the table of grace, we brought him with us. We joined our voices with his, saying in the stillness of our hearts, "Oh my, this is good. So sweet. Can I have some more?"

Sometimes the Spirit sends an unexpected angel to open us to the wonder of Christ's sustaining, trustworthy presence, and we know with goose-pimply wonder that we are in the presence of divine love in all its surprising grace-filled packages. Sometimes the sacrament of the Lord's Supper alone is enough to break through our defenses and send us to our knees in awe and wonder at the ongoing and everlasting faithfulness of

God. Sometimes it takes a special interaction, an angel unaware, to help us remember and, in remembering, rekindle our faith.

Once I was invited to speak at a ministry conference in Seoul, South Korea. It was an eventful and disorienting trip in many ways. One day the driver who was supposed to pick me up for an event forgot to come and get me. It was winter and spitting snow. I had no Korean money, but armed with my American Express card, I set off on foot to look for a restaurant. The characters of the street names confounded me, and very soon I was lost. I did not know that the restaurants were all on floors above the shops, so I was both lost and hungry.

As I stood on a street corner trying to get my bearings or find a cab, a young man came up to me and said, "You look lost. Are you OK?" His English was perfect, and I was so relieved that I poured out the whole story to him. "I know just what to do," he said. "Follow me." So I did. Down a street and up another until he pointed to an upstairs window. Lo and behold, I saw the golden arches of the McDonald's sign. He invited me up the stairs and into the restaurant, found me a table, and went off to order Big Macs for both of us.

As we ate and talked, he told me that his mother was a Christian and had been shunned by her family. His father abandoned them, but she taught him to have faith in Jesus. He was preparing to enter seminary to become a pastor. "God sent me to you," he said. "I was home watching TV, and I just knew I had to come here." I ate my tepid burger, listened to his shining faith, and thought to myself with a smile, "And I will be made known to you in the breaking of the bun." When we train the eyes of our hearts to see, we will find that the Spirit constantly sends signs, rescuers, eye-openers, and comforters to remind us that God is trustworthy and that we can rely on God's constancy.

AWAKENING TO FAITH'S GARDEN

The Spirit strengthens our faith not only in sacramental moments of clarity and the sacraments themselves, although that in itself would be enough, but also by awakening a sense of awe of creation, inspiring new insights into Scripture, and quickening our own consciences.

When faithfulness grows, we find that choices that once felt benign or inconsequential no longer seem so. When faithfulness grows, the lens through which we see the world changes. Bit by bit, we find that we see through the eyes of grace and God's values first, and through the world's skewed values and our own wounds dimly second. Overconsumption, harsh judgment, and self-centeredness become less tolerable. Apathy in the face of climate change or social injustice becomes intolerable. Why? Because faith in a trustworthy God, as it matures, makes *us* trustworthy to God. As our faithfulness grows, God entrusts us with more insight and responsibility. As we expect the Spirit to be there for us, the Spirit expects us to be there for her.

God does this strengthening directly in our hearts, through experiences of wonder and salvation. God also matures faithfulness through the power of community, particularly the faith community. It is difficult for faith to grow in isolation. It is not impossible, but it is hard. We need each other because each one of us carries a particular glimpse into the face of God and what God most loves. None are expendable. If we try to go it alone, our habits and hurts have no way to be challenged. Our joys and wonders have no way to be shared. The sparkle of the night sky glitters on all.

The nineteenth-century American evangelist D. L. Moody told a story of inviting a friend to dinner one evening. Moody had for some time been trying to get his friend to become a part of the church. The friend claimed to be a believer but did not trust organized religion and insisted he did not need it. That winter evening after dinner, the two men sat opposite each other in wing chairs in front of the fire. Moody made his case one last time to no avail.

"Why?" his friend asked. "I'm fine on my own." Moody fell silent, and the two old friends sat beside the fire together. After a while, Moody rose, and with the tongs, he took one burning coal from the fire and laid it alone on the hearth. The two of them watched it go from red to black, little by little. Neither spoke, but the next Sunday the man was in church.[13]

Faith is not just individual. It is corporate. We experience it together. We grow in faithfulness together. In the Hebrew Scriptures, God does not call only Abraham and Sarah. God calls and creates a people. Faith in Jesus is personal. But it is not merely individual. We are part of a body with many members. That is not an accidental metaphor. We need each other to live the life of Christ fully.

Granted, the church is an imperfect body filled with imperfect bodies. We can often behave in stunning, brazen, and hard-hearted ways. In the name of purity, we can crucify souls that need us most. In the name of tradition, we can wall others out. In the name of personal preference or freedom, we can hurt others' feelings with words as powerful as blows. Still, life together is not one option among many, as if we were choosing from a menu at a Chinese restaurant. Together we deepen. Together we ripen. Together we repent. Together we mend. As in all human frailties, sometimes relationships must be severed to stop the hurting or toxic patterns. Even then, we acknowledge that we have fallen short of the stature of Christ's children. Even then, God's tears water the roots of our congregations and communities, and faith rises and grows.

CONCLUSION

Nobel Prize–winning writer Rabindranath Tagore once said, "Faith is the bird that feels the light when the dawn is still dark."[14] Like Mary Magdalene on that first Easter morning, we find that we, too, must rise "while it is still dark" to do what we can for Christ, even when we are out of hope and think there is nothing we can do. That is faith. Mary Magdalene believed Jesus was dead when she gathered her cloak around her and made her way to the tomb. Even as she went, the tomb was already empty. The gift that Spirit faithfulness offers in times of pain and darkness is the promise that even when we cannot see, all that is needed has been attended to for us. *Pistis* allows us to lean into that belief when our senses and our experiences tell a different story. *Pistis,* whether quiet or clanging, always tells the story of hope. It always reminds us that behind what seems real is something that is eternally true, the love of God for us.

When I was a preschooler, I loved to stand at the front door each afternoon at 4:05. The courthouse where my father worked closed at 4:00 each day, and I waited like a panting puppy at the door, straining my ears to hear his footsteps on the porch. Most days I stood back a little from the door. When I heard the screen open, I launched at him, a bit like Keesie later launched at me. I leapt into his arms. Never once did it occur to me that he would drop me. He never did. As the fruit of faithfulness ripens in us, more and more we find that we can leap with assurance into the arms of God, trusting that we will always be caught. We will be.

A WEEK FOR TENDING
THE SHOOTS OF FAITH

Day One: "He charged them, 'This is how you shall act: in the fear of the LORD, in faithfulness, and with your whole heart'" (2 Chr. 19:9). Things are a mess in Judah. King Jehoshaphat has made too many concessions to the greedy and helped the wicked. Jehu the prophet has called him out about it, and the king is instituting reforms, especially of the judiciary. In this verse, he tells the new judges how they are to behave: with the awe of God, wholeheartedly dedicated to their job of justice, and with faithfulness as their power. In Hebrew, faithfulness means assurance or supreme confidence. What do you have wholehearted confidence in today? Does that which you depend on deserve your supreme confidence? How do you live out your confidence in God today? What does God value and promise that you can depend on? Ask God to give you wholehearted faithfulness in a way that you can feel and put to work today.

Day Two: "I have chosen the way of faithfulness; I set your ordinances before me" (Ps. 119:30). The psalmist tells us that faithfulness is not an accident or even serendipity. It is a choice. Every day we choose to rely on God's promises. As we do that, our confidence in God grows. As our confidence grows, we find that many of life's problems begin to come into new focus, and we find new and better solutions. The psalmist also reminds us that faithfulness grows when we set God's will and values before our eyes at each moment. Obedience is another choice, and it breeds deeper faithfulness. How might you live in obedience to God today? Ask in prayer if there is anything special that you can do to show your gratitude or to serve God today. Remind yourself of all the things that are important to God. Choose one of those things (service to the poor, study of Scripture, prayer, working for justice, etc.) and ask God to give you a task you can perform in that area. If something occurs to you, write it down and begin to ponder how you might fulfill that command.

Day Three: "And I came to you in weakness and in fear and in much trembling. My speech and my proclamation were made not with persuasive words of wisdom but with a demonstration of the Spirit and of power, so that your faith might rest not on human wisdom but on the power of God" (1 Cor. 2:3–5). No matter what our circumstances may be, our faithfulness is powered by God. Faith and faithfulness refer to radical reliance on God. It is trust that issues in commitment. Paul recognizes that human wisdom can take us only so far. Expecting things to make sense in the human sphere of power and posturing will not bring us the true wisdom and maturity that can come only from the Spirit. In what areas of your life do you need to trust God more? Are there things that you spend a little too much time worrying over? What, in your heart of hearts, do you fear or feel that God will not, or cannot, do for you? Take a moment to honestly tell God how you feel, even if it feels silly or you don't usually talk to God in that way. Don't worry if you don't feel anything or don't receive an "answer." The message has been received and answered. It will soon become clear. Ask God to help you trust.

Day Four: "I am hard pressed between the two: my desire is to depart and be with Christ, for that is far better, but to remain in the flesh is more necessary for you. Since I am convinced of this, I know that I will remain and continue with all of you for your progress and joy in faith" (Phil. 1:23–25). Paul is in prison. He suffers persecution and also from a terrible chronic illness or trial. In many ways, he is ready to go on and be with the Lord. Still, he realizes that he has usefulness to the churches he has founded. He wants to help them grow in trust and joy.

Those two things are integrally linked. The more we rely on Christ, the more we experience joy, even if our circumstances don't change in ways we wish. How might trusting in Christ make this a more joyful day for you? What do you need? State simply your needs before God, then practice resting in the joyful faith that God will bring to you exactly what you need, maybe even more perfectly than the requests you have made. Take a moment to imagine what it would feel like to have all your needs and yearnings fulfilled. Spend some time feeling that until it feels real. That is the state God longs for you to inhabit. Thank God for all that is coming your way.

Day Five: "And [we] sent Timothy, our brother and God's coworker in the gospel of Christ, to strengthen and encourage you for the sake of your faith" (1 Thess. 3:2). We do not have to go it alone. God wills for us to live our lives in a community of faith so that others' faith can encourage and build up our own. Who are the people in your life who encourage you and help you to trust God more? How can you give that gift to others? Look for moments throughout the day to give encouragement to yourself as well. Tell yourself that you are growing in your faith, even if you are not sure that is so. Make a renewed commitment to worship and Bible study. Ask God how you can encourage someone's faith today.

Day Six: "Woe to you, scribes and Pharisees, hypocrites! For you tithe mint, dill, and cumin and have neglected the weightier matters of the law: justice and mercy and faith. It is these you ought to have practiced without neglecting the others" (Matt. 23:23). Sometimes we major in minors, don't we? We spend our energy on small actions but do not allow faith to soften and mold our hearts. Justice and mercy are words we may not associate with faith very often. Yet they are faith's necessary partners. How does your deepening trust call you to works of justice and mercy? Make a list of those to whom you would like to offer special mercy. Ask God to give you opportunities to exercise your faithfulness in those ways.

Questions for Reflection and Discussion

1. The fruit of faith in God has its roots in God's faithfulness to us. How have you experienced God as reliable and trustworthy? Can you think of a specific story to share?
2. Faith includes trusting without reservation that you are loved without reservation. Is this difficult for you? If so, why do you think that is so? What makes it hard for you to rely on God's love for you?
3. Occasionally in the Bible the word *pistis* refers to the contents of faith or our belief systems. What are the central aspects of your belief system that help you trust in God's faithfulness in your life and in our world?
4. What are the habits of heart and mind that make faith most difficult these days? How do you see prejudice or unexamined expectations weakening faith in our day?
5. How have you experienced unexpected angels that have helped your faith? Can you think of a story to share?
6. What unleashes your faith during the storms of life?

CHAPTER 9

TENDING THE
SHOOTS OF GENTLENESS

*There is nothing so strong as gentleness, nothing
so gentle as real strength.*

—Francis de Sales

In seminary, my fabulous Old Testament professor had a deep bass voice, smoked like a fiend, and could both terrify and astound me in the space of a breath. One day after class, I was excited and confused about the day's lesson. It was the first time I had really realized that there were two very different stories of creation in Genesis—one in 1:1–2:3, and the other in 2:4–25. I was agog. I went to his desk and asked him some questions about the contradictions that I saw.

He looked at me over the half-lens glasses perched on the tip of his nose as he lit a cigarette and said, "Ambiguity is your friend, Miss Gamble, not your enemy," and walked out of the classroom. As unsatisfying as that may have felt, it is nevertheless absolutely true and a lesson we need to learn in order to ponder Spirit gentleness. The implications of this quality are vast and sometimes seem to contradict themselves.

The word Paul uses in Galatians 5:23, *prautes,* is fascinating and nearly untranslatable. It refers to our inner attitude toward God in which, from the very core of who we are, we accept God's dealings with us, God's very self, as good. Therefore, we live our lives without disputing or resisting. Wow!

Spirit gentleness is not, as we often use the word today, practiced shyness or milquetoast wishy-washiness. It is not, as we say in the South, "being sweet." Rather than a word that connotes weakness in any way, *prautes* connotes power. It is the big power that comes from the knowledge that all the resources of God are being brought to bear in every circumstance, so we don't have to be unduly upset all the time.

Prautes in ordinary Greek is the word used for an animal that has been brought under control, trusts the leader, and therefore can relax in the feeling of security and knowing its place in things. When we got our dog Bonnie from the shelter, she had been a stray. She didn't know how to climb stairs or walk on a leash. She was especially wild on walks, and I suffered several falls in those first days. One early morning, I took her out and she bolted. I hit the ground hard. As I lay there dazed, something seemed to click in her. She came back and sat next to me. It was as if she realized that if I was hurt, she was in big trouble, so she had better smarten up. From that time on, she began to accept the leash. While she is still not in love with it, she knows that her life is better with it because she trusts that I have her best interest at heart. *Prautes.* I don't have to resist, because I trust the one holding the lead.

The opposite of *prautes* is self-promotion, self-interest, and self-aggrandizement. *Prautes* results in an inner calmness that is neither elated nor deflated because it is simply not occupied with itself at all. It doesn't have to be. This Spirit quality matures from the unassailable certainty that God is God, God is good, and God is always up to something good.

Prautes is possible in us because the Spirit indwells us. It is possible because, as all the aspects of the fruit are, it is who the Spirit is: always good, always active, always compassionate, always doing the right and appropriate thing.

SPIRIT GENTLENESS IN THE BIBLE

In the Hebrew Bible, words translated as "gentle" generally carry a sense of tenderness, devotion, compliance, delicacy, or compassion. Proverbs 15:4 says, "A gentle tongue is a tree of life, but perverseness in it breaks the spirit." In that verse, the opposite of gentleness is contrariness that takes a spiritual toll. In Jeremiah 11:19, the prophet says, "I was like a gentle lamb led to the slaughter." This connotes trusting innocence that could not, or would not, protect itself. In Psalm 18:35, the same word is translated as "help" when the psalmist extols God's salvation and support that has elevated him in time of trouble.

In the messianic prophecies of the Suffering Servant in Isaiah, the messiah is oppressed and silently suffering, "like a lamb that is led to the slaughter" (Isa. 53:7). There is a poignant nonviolent, non-retaliatory quality to these images. Images of a compassionately powerful God overflow in the beautiful poem of comfort that is the Twenty-third Psalm. There God tends, guides, leads, and protects, without faltering, in times of trial and trouble. Isaiah uses similar images of shepherding in chapter 40.

In Deuteronomy 8, Israel is reminded of how the God of powerful gentleness led them through the wilderness. God's tender, loving, wise, compassionate gentleness reaches its pinnacle on Mount Sinai when God offers Moses a love letter like no other (the Ten Commandments) in which God declares God's love and shares God's desires for how people can live fully with one another. A through line in those sacred words is God's yearning to protect people from harm and from harming one another.

Gentleness as tenderness and reasonableness finds its way into the New Testament with a different Greek word, *epieikeia*. That word refers to something that is fitting, equitable, fair, moderate, forbearing, not insistent on the letter of the law. Someone who expresses this characteristic shows evenhanded consideration. A version of this word was used to characterize a nurse with trying children or a teacher with difficult students. Some translate the word "sweet reasonableness." It is marked by considerateness and humane behavior. *Prautes* is a bit different.

In the New Testament, *prautes* is used in three basic ways. First, it is used to express being conformable to the will of God. We see this sense in Matthew 5:5, "Blessed are the meek [*prautes*], for they will inherit the earth." Jesus reminds us here that when we conform ourselves to God's values, including *prautes*, that is where real power lies. It is not to be found in the world's power structures but in God. Also in Matthew, Jesus reminds us that his way is the way of *prautes*. In Matthew 11:28–29, he calls us to come to him when we are heavy laden and tells us that he himself is gentle (*praus*) and will provide rest to those who answer the call. His *prautes* is not rocked by what rocks us. It is centered and comfortable with what is. He paints a beautiful picture of a walk of life in which we model ourselves on his own gentleness (*prautes*). Being conformable, modeling our lives on Jesus' gentle confidence, is where rest from burdens lies.

Second, the word means "to be teachable." In James 1:21, the author uses a form of *prautes* to tell us not to be too proud to humbly learn from the word implanted within us. *Prautes* opens up the soul and makes it malleable. If our responses to challenge are no longer programmed by fight or flight, by severing relationship or seeking revenge, then there is room in us to learn more about ourselves and God. When we become more teachable, we become more usable.

Most often *prautes* is used, as in Galatians, to describe power-infused consideration that rests solely on trust in the constant goodness of God. While patience helps us curb anger when provoked, gentleness allows us to reject aggression. Aristotle saw *prautes* as referring to the middle ground between excessive anger and excessive angerlessness. He called it a golden mean between extremes. He saw it as the quality of a person who is always angry at the right time and never at the wrong time. When just a seedling in our souls, Spirit gentleness is not so much a settled disposition as it is a conscious choice that, over time, transforms the lens through which we view the world and the self. Finding the most fitting response in difficult circumstances is hard work and not for the fainthearted or wishy-washy. It requires the capacity to choose our responses rather than reacting with first emotions.

PESTS IN THE
GARDEN OF GENTLENESS

Spirit gentleness is rooted in trust that God is good, God's ways are good, and God's dealings with God's people and all creation are unfailingly good. Most of us accept that truth as a matter of faith or dogma. It is not always a settled disposition in our hearts, however. We look at the wreckage of war, gun violence, and calcified divisions and sometimes wonder if God is good or has just given up on us.

After the massacre at Columbine High School in Littleton, Colorado, back in our more innocent days when some of us still thought that kind of violence was an aberration, a friend who was achingly trying to claw his way to faith wrote me a simple email: "Eugenia, if God, why Littleton?"

Of course, gun violence is not caused by God. Still, in the intervening years, now nearly a quarter of a century, those kinds of questions are often asked by both believers and seekers in times of shock and powerlessness. Where is God? And is God good?

The problem of evil is as old as time. How does God permit it? Is God the author of it? In the garden, after their refusal to live with healthy boundaries, Adam and Eve hid themselves because they were afraid of God. Would God lash out in anger? Would God return evil for evil? Was God still good when humans did something willfully bad? God's response answers that question tenderly. God expresses sorrow, even confusion, in the presence of their disobedience and the flimsy fig leaves behind which they hope to hide. God sews more substantial clothes for them from animal skins (Gen. 3:21) so that they will not have to always be confronted by the shame and vulnerability of their betrayal. Still, they fear, as we sometimes do, that because they had messed up, God was going to do something awful to them.

It can be argued that sending them from the garden into a life of laboring both for a living and to deliver new generations was the action of an angry and vengeful God. But was it? Is doing something hard but meaningful somehow a curse? Ask a pastor on Easter morning or a mother when she first holds her newborn. Is working the land a curse or a previously unknown blessing? Are labor pains a curse or an intimate sharing with God of the power of creation itself? Is death, and the fear of it, a curse or a portal? It depends on how you view God. And how we really view God is not solely a matter of how we think we view God.

It is easy for many of us to trust in God's goodness when things are going well—when we get the promotion, or our child gets a scholarship, or the biopsy comes back clean. Our response then is often, "God is so good!" But what happens when the relationship with our spouse disintegrates despite our fervent prayers, or our child is arrested, or the dreaded call comes in the night, or we lose our job, or our body does not heal? What happens when we sit on the dung heap with Job, see nothing but loss everywhere we look, and nothing seems to work anymore? One of my cousins, after a painful divorce, wrote a poem about it that contains a phrase that has stuck with me for decades, "all my stuff was not enough." What happens then?

That is when we seem to need the powerful gentleness of *prautes* most and have access to it least. Job's friends were no help to him as he sat in the devastations of his shattered life. They just wanted to lay blame somewhere, fix the problem, or—if all else failed—have him curse God and die. But some sacred how, Job did none of that. He sat with his threadbare faith, clung to it when he could not feel it, acted from it when his strength was dried up and when answers were like vapors. He sat there. He waited. He trusted, and even when he couldn't trust anymore, he trusted anyway that somehow God was real. Somehow God was good. Somehow God was up to good. The book of Job is not so much a story of what happens when bad things happen to good people. It is a story about what it might take to break one's faith that God is good when nothing good is happening anywhere you can see.

"If God, why Littleton?" "How could a good God allow the Holocaust?" "How could a good and sovereign God allow children to be born with horrible deformities or to die in their cribs or to starve before age five?" "How could a good God promise protection, and my child died in her elementary classroom?" "How could a good God seem to smite some who have done nothing wrong, like Job, and unreasonably wink and turn away from others who commit adultery, murder, and dance naked in the streets, like King David?" "How can you read the Bible and think God is good when he is shown as petty, vindictive, rageful, and unfair?" All of those are actual questions that have been asked of me through tears, or with clenched fists, over the years.

The theological effort to vindicate divine goodness in light of the existence of evil is called theodicy, and in my view, it has not offered a whole lot of help. No matter how hard we push and tug, the mystery of God's sovereignty and goodness on one hand and devastating evil on the other remain difficult to reconcile neatly. So these questions from our own lives remain and must be wrestled out just as Job had to do, just as Abraham had to do, just as Jesus had to do in the garden of betrayal or as he drowned in his own blood on the cross. Can we, when times are excruciating, relax into the arms of a good God? Can we find within ourselves the power of acceptance? Can we allow Spirit gentleness to hold sway even over our pain and fear? It is not easy, but it is possible.

WEEDS IN THE
GARDEN OF GENTLENESS

In addition to deepening our belief that God really is good, in order for Spirit gentleness to mature, we need to realize that there are attitudes and mind-sets that are poisonous to it. Prejudice in any form makes gentleness nearly impossible to grow. Why? Because the referent for all prejudice is ourselves. We don't like this person, or we are offended by that person, or we are afraid of those people, so they must be controlled. When we nurse our prejudices, before we know it, we ourselves become the sun around which the whole earth orbits. We can become toxically protective of what we decide are our rights or the outcomes we insist on. There is no room for gentleness when we are certain we are right about everything at all times and that it is our job to insist that others align with our views or else be shunned.

Spirit gentleness with its steady reliance on the goodness of God cannot flourish when our points of view become our gods and everyone who disagrees becomes an enemy that is expendable. Gentleness involves the capacity to remain calm and centered even in the face of hostility or confusion. We cannot be gentle when we see enemies everywhere. When we nurse prejudice, the ground of our hearts becomes hard, and we are not open to possibilities and often decide that animosity is justified. Prejudice is the ultimate narcissism. It leads to either-or thinking. Gentleness arises from both-and thinking.

Unfettered anger and blame are also weeds that will strangle out gentleness. Remember that anger itself is not sinful. In Ephesians 4:25–26, the author reminds us that in the new life of Christ, anger has its place. We sometimes need anger to move gospel imperatives forward. Jesus himself showed some truly blistering moments of anger in the face of injustice (John 2:13–17) and when dealing with the hypocrisy of the religious establishment (Matt. 23). In Ephesians 4:26, the author says, "Be angry but do not sin." That is the balance that *prautes* requires.

What makes anger sinful? When anger is selfish, vindictive, unmoored from the values of God, or simply free-floating and looking for a victim, that is sin. It is one thing to be angry in the presence of injustice or personal attack. It is another thing to feel attacked in general, take an assault rifle, and shoot people you don't know at the bank, church, or grocery store. When our anger becomes free-floating, ravening, and looking for a victim, any victim, it will not only crowd out Spirit gentleness but also convince us that gentleness is weakness and that only force makes right. Beneath that kind of anger is a wound that must be healed for life to be anything like whole. It has been said that anger is just sadness's bodyguard. It can also be guarding fear, shame, pain, loneliness, or lack of meaning. Aggression is the answer to none of those things.

One other gentleness killer is resistance to anything that feels personally threatening but that in actuality is not harmful, only unfamiliar or scary. In that regard, what we resist persists and becomes magnified in importance. The resistance practiced in the Spirit's garden is staunch opposition to evil. Scripture gives us whole body armor with which to do that work (Eph. 6:10–17). The Hebrew prophets were masters of resistance in the face of evil and oppression. Jesus resisted hypocrisy, prejudice, and the status quo. That type of resistance is often a manifestation of Spirit kindness or goodness.

The nonresistance that is at the heart of gentleness, however, has more to do with allowing ourselves to become pliable in God's hands. It has to do with openness and humility as opposed to legalism and rigidity. The nonresistance that is part of gentleness creates inner space in which we can respond without retaliation, with humility, and with quiet steady wisdom to situations that are new and triggering. When Spirit gentleness arises in us, we do not fight our circumstances. We face them and respond in ways that acknowledge that God is with us, within us, and among us.

TENDING THE ROOTS OF GENTLENESS

Spirit gentleness is one of the most needed aspects of the fruit of the Spirit in days of agitation, injustice, and systemic lies. It is a quality that allows us not to sink into despair but, rather, to take a breath and view situations from a broader perspective. Spirit gentleness does not rise from determination. It arises from awakening. When we are displaying gentleness, we cease comparisons that breed jealousy, contempt, or self-righteousness. We see with breathless clarity that we are a part of something bigger than ourselves that has our back and is moving us in a positive direction. Even if that direction takes us, like the phoenix, through the flames of disintegration, we will always rise. God's goodness always prevails. When Spirit gentleness flows through us, we become aware that there is an essential unity to all creation, even in our blessed diversity. We are one because God is One. And we have been gifted with the Spirit's own capacity to make choices in light of this reality. This capacity is truly exquisite. It is also difficult and fleeting. It both requires and results in inner freedom.

Desert mystics called the process of moving toward inner freedom and balance detachment. To be free to be gentle, we release the hold that outcomes, strategies, and distractions have on our emotions and energies. Letting go is not the same thing as giving up. It is not throwing up our hands in helplessness. It is choosing, and acknowledging, power where it actually lies.

Spirit gentleness reminds us that there may be a better and more grace-filled outcome than we can currently see. God always provides alternatives and pathways through any pain or devastation. Was Abraham's invitation to return Isaac to God a test of his faith? The text would support that view. I wonder, though, if it was more opportunity than final exam. Perhaps it was an opportunity to experience not only the power of his trust in God's goodness but also the creativity of God's bigger plan. Perhaps Abraham needed to experience the power of his own attachments, the bonds of his desires, the terror of his love for his son, in order to find a steady trust that could lead him to freedom. I know that has often been true for me. The value of this traumatic story may be in reminding us that God is at work in even the worst of circumstances to display goodness and call us to a wider understanding.

Gentleness like this can feel quite uncomfortable because when we enter into it fully we are not in control and our hearts are vulnerable. Often our own blind spots are mirrored back to us when we choose the way of gentleness. Gentleness may not be reciprocated. We may be attacked as weak or dismissed as being lazy or manipulative. Even if that is the case, each time we choose to respond from gentleness we will learn more about ourselves, our resistances, and our own petty judgments. Choosing to live from a balanced, detached, big-picture, uncontentious reasonableness is not a value in our aggrieved culture. But it is an ultimate value in the Spirit's garden.

The wonderful spiritual writer James Finley cautions that we have to be careful not to become attached to becoming detached. That is just another addiction. It can also become a safe refuge for cowardice. The kind of release that is needed for gentleness to sprout and grow has seasons, as every garden does. It comes in waves that slowly unfold. Detachment can feel like losing, but it is more like clearing the ground so that the abundant deeper wonders of life in Christ can rise. If we think of detachment like pulling a barnacle off an oyster shell, it will seem impossible and damaging. But if we allow the Spirit to lead the way, confident that a good path will be revealed as we chip away at the hard stuff, gentleness will push its shoots up in the soil of our soul when needed most.

Spirit gentleness arises best from the ground of humility. Many of us have known the long loneliness of constantly trying to win and be right about everything. That does little but leave us a bundle of nerve endings reacting instinctively to everything that may seem a threat. Gentleness knows that it doesn't know everything, see everything, or need to win everything. There is an exquisite smallness to Spirit gentleness, like a perfect snowflake that needs to be nothing other than what it is. Ripening gentleness releases the notion of winning over another, defeating another, or ascending over another, because the other is exactly like us, and when we encounter others, we find God asking to be let in. Augustine once advised that Christians never fight evil as if it were something that arose totally outside ourselves. That is not to say that it arises entirely within us, either. It is just to say that there is really no part of us that is completely free of the taint of toxic ego. Gentleness, therefore, requires the disconcerting reorientation of mind that chooses to put itself in others' shoes while remaining grounded in the certainty of God's goodness.

CONCLUSION

This is the shortest chapter in the book, perhaps because this characteristic of the fruit is often so lacking in my life and in our world. Perhaps its very elusiveness contains its allure. We are tired of struggle, choosing sides, and naming enemies. We are exhausted from the daily onslaught of evil and pain in the world. God understands this and offers us the invitation to dip into Spirit gentleness as medicine and motivation when times are hard.

The capacity to choose our responses to life from a stance of balanced, trusting reasonableness is a powerful fruit of our deepening trust that God is good. Just because God is good does not mean that all people are up to good all the time, even though we are made in God's image. Not everything that God's people are convinced is God's will is, in fact, God's will. We are all little packages of contradictions.

We are capable of great love, elegance, and openness. We are also capable of mortifying smallness, meanness, and parsimony. We are capable of wisdom, insight, and sublime experiences of the holy. And we are capable of blasphemy, infamy, and heresy in the space of a heartbeat.

The Spirit fruit of gentleness, when nurtured intentionally, gives us the power to choose what is right and best in any circumstance. It gives us the capacity to choose to mirror God's goodness, compassion, steadfastness, and clarity in a world that has forgotten to notice those things. Gentleness allows us, as God did for Adam and Eve, to sew sturdy aprons even for those who have hurt and disappointed us most, because we ourselves are not the subject of every sentence. Gentleness allows us to rest in the knowledge that God is bigger, finer, and more compassionate than we know. As we practice that resting, we, too, become bigger, finer, and more compassionate than we have dreamed possible.

A WEEK FOR
TENDING GENTLENESS

Day One: "For I will leave in the midst of you a people humble and lowly. They shall seek refuge in the name of the LORD" (Zeph. 3:12). Zephaniah has just warned the people of the destruction they face at the hands of their enemies. As is common in the Hebrew Bible, the prophets equate Israel's suffering and defeats with its shallow and halfhearted faith. Here the prophet gives a word of comfort. All is not lost; the meek or gentle will remain. This kind of meekness is not weakness; it is, rather, profound strength that comes from relying on God. In what ways might you take refuge in God this week? Are there areas of your life in which you feel vulnerable or disappointed? Stop often today and repeat this prayer: "Today I take refuge in you, O Lord." Repeat it often, even if the statement feels more aspirational than a matter of fact. The prayer itself will open up a new reliance and strength in you.

Day Two: "Come to me, all you who are weary and are carrying heavy burdens, and I will give you rest. Take my yoke upon you, and learn from me, for I am gentle and humble in heart, and you will find rest for your souls. For my yoke is easy, and my burden is light" (Matt. 11:28–30). Gentleness is an inward grace of the soul. Here Jesus uses the word to describe himself and to help us understand the level of peace and rest that he offers to us. Are there areas of your life in which you feel less than peaceful and rested? Take a moment to list those areas in a prayerful attitude before God. Then offer each to God with a gentle prayer of thanks. For example: "Dear God, I am worn out from trying to make things work out. Give me peace and rest, for I know that you are always working good for me in this area of my life." Try throughout the day to notice when you feel frustrated, overwhelmed, or worried. In each instance, pause and offer the situation to God, trusting that God is working something wonderful for you long before you see it.

Day Three: "Blessed are the meek, for they will inherit the earth" (Matt. 5:5). Here Jesus tells us that the inward disposition of powerful acceptance of God's goodness and trustworthiness is at the heart of happiness (the meaning of the word "blessed"). Not only is our joy tied to our gentleness, but living out our gentleness makes us like God and heirs of all the richness and beauty of the earth itself. What a powerfully wonderful promise! Because Jesus describes himself as gentle, when we act in gentle acceptance of God's goodness and love for us, we are acting like the body of Christ itself. Ponder today how you might practice deeper acceptance of God's goodness in your life. Let your heart remind you of all the good things that God has done for you. Don't try too hard. Just let the thoughts and blessings come into your mind. Don't "yes, but" them. Let yourself feel the feelings of joy associated with those blessings as if they were all happening to you right now. When you are doing your daily duties, pause often to pray: "I am filled with blessing. I am filled with joy. All that you have for me, Lord, I am receiving in due time."

Day Four: "I, therefore, the prisoner in the Lord, beg you to walk in a manner worthy of the calling to which you have been called, with all humility and gentleness, with patience, bearing with one another in love" (Eph. 4:1–2). Gentle and powerful acceptance of our situations is difficult enough in good times. For some of us, it is nearly impossible in times of trial. Paul was in prison, and still he accepted that even in the horror, God was working out that which was good and perfect for him. This kind of gentleness is possible because it does not rely on our own power. It is rooted entirely in God's power and goodness. Paul is experiencing this for himself in horrible circumstances, and so he urges the church in Ephesus to deepen its dependence on Christ in order to withstand whatever is coming its way. Can you identify anyone in your life who has shown you this kind of gentleness and faith during hard times? What is your usual response to hardship? What helps make it bearable for you? How do you connect to God in times of difficulty? Remember in prayer today all the faithful who are living with trials or under persecution. Ask God to fill each one with gentle assurance of God's goodness and love.

Day Five: "As God's chosen ones, holy and beloved, clothe yourselves with compassion, kindness, humility, meekness, and patience" (Col. 3:12). Here we learn that the graces are ours to control in life. We may put them on like a sweater against the winter chill or a sun hat in the summer sun. It is not too hard for us. We have them already in our spiritual closet, carefully chosen and a perfect fit for us. We simply need to pick them up and put them on. Another implication of the clothing language is that the graces we wear will be visible to others. While *prautes* is primarily an inward attitude of the soul toward God, living out that attitude shows to the world. It is patently obvious. Which of the graces in this verse do you think is most obvious in your life? How do you think that others notice your gentle, confident trust in God? When you get dressed this morning, or put on a jacket or sweater later in the day or a robe at night, take a moment to say to yourself: I am wearing my gentle trust in God's goodness today. Notice how you feel and whether you can see a difference in how you act or react today as a result of "wearing" your faith.

Day Six: "But as for you, man of God, shun all this; pursue righteousness, godliness, faith, love, endurance, gentleness" (1 Tim. 6:11). Paul is writing to his discouraged colleague Timothy. His letter is full of practical advice for his ministry. He is cautioning him not to give in to the temptation of looking to wealth to solve problems or to be an end in and of itself. Instead, he is to pursue the things that really make life worth living. One of those things is gentleness. While gentleness is a result of living by the Spirit, we must pursue this level of faith and acceptance actively to receive full benefit. How might you pursue gentleness today? In what areas can you seek to trust God more? How can you make God's goodness known today? Try to think of one specific action (large or small) and commit to it today (not tomorrow). If you are at a loss for how you might pursue *prautes,* ask God to bring an obvious opportunity to you. In the meantime, go over in your mind all the things that you love and that bring you joy. As you are reminded of, and feel, all of that, your gentle, powerful trust will grow as well.

Questions for Reflection and Discussion

1. How would you respond to someone who questions whether God is good in light of the world's ills? Do you have a story of God's goodness that you can share?
2. What allows you to hold fast to God's goodness in times of trouble? What makes it difficult for you?
3. How do you respond to Aristotle's definition of *prautes*? Can you think of times in your life when you exercised that perfect middle ground between reactivity and passivity?
4. What is your understanding of spiritual detachment? How is that different from apathy?
5. What are the situations that make *prautes* difficult in our world? What might help? How do you think that this quality might address the divisions and aggressions that are so common?
6. Gentleness refuses to let the faults of others define their lives or worth. How does this understanding shape our concepts of enemy or opponent? Notice if any prejudices arise in your heart as you think about this.

CHAPTER 10

TENDING THE
SHOOTS OF SELF-CONTROL

Where you stumble, there your treasure lies.
—Joseph Campbell

My favorite movie, *Chariots of Fire*, was released in the United States when I was in seminary in 1982. The movie centers around the British men's track team as they prepare for and run in the 1924 Olympic games in France. I remember sitting huddled in the worn seats of the small campus movie house watching those men train and marveling at how disciplined they were. Their drive and self-mastery amazed me as a young woman who had, even then, spent her whole life dragging her challenging body behind her energetic spirit.

Still, it was not the physical mastery of the athletes that seared that movie into my heart with such force that forty years later I wept uncontrollably when I saw it. It was the moral strength. One of the central characters in the film is a young Scotsman, Eric Liddell. Liddell was devout in the strict old-school Presbyterian tradition. He was a preacher who later became a missionary in China, where he died during World War II. But in *Chariots,* he is young, strong, and centered.

His true strength is put to the test when a heat is scheduled to be run on a Sunday. Liddell, who kept Sabbath holy by worshiping and resting, refuses to run, knowing that in so doing he will likely lose his chance at a medal. The Prince of Wales, the prime minister, and other high officials call Liddell in for a meeting to try to persuade him that duty to country is of a higher order than a Sabbath practice. They try without success to find a way for Liddell to make it right within himself to run and to win the gold for Britain. Liddell wants to run. He wants that medal. He feels as if all that he had sacrificed and trained for is going to be lost, but he will not budge. Eventually another runner offers his place to Liddell so that he can run on another day, and indeed he wins the medal. After the confrontation in the great rooms of power, one member of the House of Lords says to the prime minister, "Thank God that there is someone left who will not sell his soul, even for his country."

Self-control is not simply mastery of the body, its impulses, or even the ego. It is more than restraint that can be momentary and full of delusion. It is not the self-righteous feeling of power that comes from choosing not to have a second scoop of ice cream when you get home from the doctor's office where you have been told, once again, to lose some weight. It is not the teeth-gritted determination to give up doughnuts for Lent only to find yourself on Easter morning, not at the sunrise service, but at the back of a long line at the Krispy Kreme drive-through. Spirit self-control is the capacity to regularly choose actions that are consistent with one's truest values and are consistent with who God is and what God values. It is not about self-denial. It is about freedom.

The word that Paul uses in his list in Galatians 5 describing what Spirit produces in believers is *enkrateia*. It is one of a number of Greek words that we translate into English as strength, ability, force, or might. Each has a slightly different nuance of meaning. The root of this word, *kratos,* means strength, force, the capacity to hold fast to something in difficult circumstances, to maintain or retain that which is valuable, to exercise dominion or mastery over something, or to have the power to hold everything together. Self-*kratos* is the capacity to do all those things within the self and on behalf of a greater good. It is to master one's own soul, ego, and impulses in order to hold fast to what is best, to maintain a centered spirit, to hold life together as a sacred whole through the daily choices one makes. It is about the right use of our ability to make choices.

Spirit self-control harnesses the tyrannical wounded ego that wants what it wants when it wants it, regardless of the consequences that may result from trying to get it or from actually having it. Self-control is about saying no to self when saying yes would be harmful or hurtful. And it is about saying yes when saying no would be easier or somehow damaging. It is not an end in itself. Self-control's goal is the majestic freedom that arises from a heart that is no longer ruthlessly driven by immediate desires. Self-control arises when consequences beyond the moment become real and we refuse any action that causes harm. It creates room in the soul for us to live with a new awareness of God's presence and ways. Self-control results in a life of non-needy moderation. The opposite of *enkrateia* in biblical Greek is *akrates,* which means powerless, morally impotent, and unrestrained.

SELF-CONTROL IN THE BIBLE

The English term "self-control" appears only once in the Old Testament. In Proverbs 25:28, the wisdom writer says, "Like a city breached, without walls, is one who lacks self-control." The Hebrew word used here is *matsar.* It means control, rule, or restraint. This word associates self-control with strong boundaries within which real safety resides.

The concept of self-control appears in several Old Testament stories, though the writers do not name it as such. In Genesis 39, after being sold into slavery in Egypt by his brothers, Joseph makes himself useful to his master Potiphar. Things go well until Potiphar's wife takes a shine to Joseph and repeatedly begs him to sleep with her. Joseph shows self-control in refusing her and fleeing from her advances. Insulted by this, she makes up stories about him to her husband, who throws Joseph into prison. Exercising self-control can have powerful, sometimes negative, consequences. Still, when it is exercised with an eye toward the greater good, God will, as God does for Joseph, find a way to turn negative circumstances around.

More often, the Old Testament offers stories of self-control by showing characters' lack of it and the dire consequences that result. King David, acting on his overwhelming desire to possess the married Bathsheba, sets in motion consequences that cause pain and death for himself and his children. When Sarah cannot control her jealousy of the enslaved Hagar and her son with Abraham, her lack of self-control leads to pain for the outcasts that only God could turn around.

In the New Testament, self-control appears in several lists of character traits of Christians. In the short letter of encouragement to Titus, the word occurs five times (1:8; 2:2, 5, 6, 12). Paul lists it among the qualities of sound doctrine, explicitly urging self-control on the young but also for the old, whom he calls to be temperate, prudent, chaste, and loving in their households.

In his letters to the church in Corinth, Paul writes to a church torn apart by competing ethical stances on business practices, fund-raising, and sexual expression. In 1 Corinthians 7:5–9, Paul tells them about the need for self-control in matters of sex. He tells wives and husbands not to withhold sexual relations from each other, except by mutual agreement for short periods in order to devote themselves to prayer. He tells them that if they abstain too long, it will give Satan an opportunity to exploit their lack of self-control. He expresses the hope that the unmarried and widows will remain chaste, but if they can't control themselves, they should marry, because the flames of untamed passion can cause so much damage.

In Paul's own life story in Acts 24, he experiences how devastating the response to the call for mastery of emotions, diligence, and self-control can be. Charges are brought against him as a rabble-rouser who is too persistent (a quality of self-control) and causes nothing but trouble in the temple and the community. The governor Felix, unsettled by Paul, imprisons him. While Paul is in jail, Felix and his wife, Drusilla, send for him, and he speaks to them about "justice, self-control, and the coming judgment" (24:25). The coupling of justice with self-control and accountability terrifies Felix, and he remands Paul to prison, where he remains for the remainder of Felix's tenure. Even so, Felix sends for him often to talk about these things.

Self-control that is rooted in a sustaining faith can be both alluring and terrifying at the same time. It is not a quality that many truly embody. So when we are in the presence of a centered, valiant, self-controlled person, even an imperfect one, we experience a kind of luminosity that calls and repels because it so radically changes the status quo.

SELF-CONTROL AND THE WORKS OF THE FLESH

In his correspondence with his churches, Paul recognizes the necessity of coherence in a believer's life. What we do is what we declare. As Francis of Assisi is widely reported to have said, "Preach the Gospel everywhere at all times. Use words if you have to." It is this coherence that leads to freedom. Eventually.

Freedom is the main subject of the Letter to the Galatians and the context for its articulation of the fruit of the Spirit (5:22–23). Leading up to these verses, Paul reminds us that spiritual freedom is both from something and for something. When the people of Israel were freed *from* slavery in Egypt, they were freed *to* a new life in a land of promise. Being released from bondage into freedom is a journey that takes as long as it takes. As we saw with the Israelites in the wilderness, it can even take generations.

In Galatians, Paul makes clear that being free from bondage to the law is not license to do anything one pleases. In chapter 5, Paul offers a picture of two ways of life. The first is the life of the flesh, with its by-products called "works of the flesh." This term does not refer only to the physical aspects of life. It refers to all human beings' sinful and exploitative impulses, tendencies, and inclinations. Before he tells us what Spirit fruit looks like and does, Paul tells us what it does not.

In verses 19–21, Paul lists a stream of inappropriate and sinful behaviors that are incompatible with the Spirit's life and fruit. These words need careful examination as we think about where, and in what circumstances, Paul thought self-control might be most needed.

Let's look at each of the words Paul chooses. He says that these behaviors are *obvious*. That word means to flaunt oneself. There is no disguising ourselves when we are serving "the world." That devotion will always be obvious, not least in a divided heart. *Sexual immorality* literally means prostitution but includes sexual vice and adultery. It is used particularly in connection with religious rituals common to the pagan practices of the time. The problem was not sex per se. It was the wrong beliefs that inspired the behavior. *Impurity* refers to anything that defiles or divides the heart and distracts from right living. *Debauchery* refers to conduct, sometimes sexual, sometimes not, that is marked by unrestrained violence and willfulness. Rape would be an example of this, as would any type of torture—physical or emotional.

Idolatry is considered the root of all the other sins. This word means giving something other than God the status of God, with the result that when faced with a choice, we will follow the idol's leading. *Sorcery*, literally the use of drugs, was associated with witchcraft. *Enmities* refers to hatred and hard feelings that belittle, create fear, and lead to retaliation. It is the opposite of friendship. *Strife* refers to disturbances of relationships that grow out of a spirit of competition and out-of-hand ambition. *Jealousy* is a specific term referring to a process that begins with devotion, loyalty, and zeal toward the loved person or object. It then moves to anger and rage when a threat is perceived, and it finally results in a malignant possessiveness that will stop at nothing. *Anger* refers to hot flashes of rage that are easily provoked. *Quarrels* refers to bickering from selfish ambition. These are the kind of quarrels that are designed to make another look and feel small. *Dissensions* refers to infighting within the body. *Factions*, literally "party spirit," refers to behaviors that are ruled by the desire for power and recognition.

Envy couples desires with malice. *Drunkenness* is plural in this verse and refers to repeated episodes, habitual intoxication. It was considered a problem in the ancient world because it was believed to reduce humans to the status of beasts and dulled the senses to the goodness of God. It weakened self-control while numbing one to the leading of the Spirit. *Carousing* refers to loud, drunken parties that disturb the peace.

Paul says that if we do those things, then we "will not inherit the kingdom of God." There is more to unpack there than the scope of this chapter permits, but in general, Paul is saying that these behaviors are signs of a lifestyle ruled by something other than God. It is not a single instance of sin that results in forfeiture of the status of children of God. It is a lifestyle marked by these choices that overruns the Spirit's garden and leads to disaster. These behaviors and the fruit of the Spirit cannot occupy the same ground at the same time. In ending his list of qualities of the fruit with self-control, Paul reminds us that we are not helpless in the presence of our worst impulses. We have Spirit power that we can employ to deal with them.

Self-control is not egotistic self-centeredness. It is usually the opposite. If we look at this list of works of the flesh, we see that at the heart of each is a self-centered willingness to exploit, use, or disregard the sacred worth of other people or groups. The word "sacrilege" means to take possession of the sacred (another person, ourselves, our power) and to use it for one's own ends rather than to reverence it. When the ego self is in control, sacrilege is inevitable. It is all about me, me, me, now, now, now.

SIN AND SELF-CONTROL

Sin is actually an attempt to cope in unsuitable ways. Perhaps you do not feel prone to any of the behaviors that Paul lists. It is not an exhaustive list, any more than the list of fruit contains all that the Spirit produces. Part of Paul's purpose in putting the works of the flesh up front is to shake people into wakefulness. We have to know the worst of our capabilities before we experience the heights of the Spirit's capabilities. In listing the works of the flesh, Paul effectively says, This is what is rotting your roots. This is why you are restless, guilt ridden, and lonely. This is why you are constantly looking for anesthesia: because you have decided that anything is acceptable if it makes you feel better. Temporarily.

Sin is whatever stops the flow of the Spirit in us. The weeds in the garden are the result of a dammed-up flow. Each instance of sin is a lost opportunity to love, and we pay a price for that. Remember that sin is always chosen. We could have made a different choice.

Over the years, I have come to realize that I am rarely punished *for* my sin. I am punished *by* it, by the memory of it or the consequences unleashed. God does not stop loving and forgiving. The Spirit does not stop offering and opening. But I contract. I become small, feel afraid, and spend my energy on creating elaborate masks that dam up the Spirit's winsome flow within me. In that condition, I often wind up fearing the darkness *and* the light in myself and the world. Perhaps that is your experience sometimes as well. When it is, we will do just about anything, use any person, to convince ourselves that the darkness is *out there,* not *in* us, and all our problems are somebody else's fault. We will also do just about anything not to see the truth about our lies. And so one choice becomes another, and a cycle becomes a lifestyle.

To effectively deal with sinful behaviors, we quickly learn that we can't fight sin with sin. If we try to do that, we discover that what we fight directly, we often mirror. One of the things that is so lastingly amazing about leaders like Dr. Martin Luther King Jr. and Rep. John Lewis is their steadfast refusal to fight violence with violence and hate with hate. It takes a mighty degree of self-mastery to heed Paul's warning in Romans 12:17, "Do not repay anyone evil for evil."

Many of us fail this test when the stakes are highest, in the toil of peacemaking or justice work or even intimacy in our own relationships. One of the most hostile groups I've ever been with was a group of faithful people at a peacemaking conference. It is so easy to become what we most despise when we feel threatened and helpless. It doesn't take long for a right action done with wrong energy to become a wrong action. Only the Spirit's fruit of mature self-control can protect us from descending to the level of our unjust opponents.

This doesn't happen only in the big fights of our times and culture. It also happens around the breakfast table or when doing the ordinary tasks of intimacy, such as monitoring our spending, saving for a vacation, assigning blame when things don't go well or our feelings get hurt. My father once said to me, "Genie, always think three consequences ahead of your mouth." He was a master of self-control himself and recognized early that his young daughter had some maturing to do in that regard.

In Reformed theology, sin is not contained in a laundry list of forbidden choices. Those choices are a result of sin, not the totality of sin itself. Sin is an attitude, a disposition, in which ego rules and rebels against the good. Calvin called this total depravity, which just means that there is nothing in us that is completely free from the taint of self-serving broken ego. If we examine even our noblest aspirations and purest loves, there is in them at least a hint of desire for reciprocation that can taint our loving choices if not mastered.

Because we are all unique, the stumbling blocks for each of us will be different, but the results will be the same. Love will grow cold, and we will not see the fruit of the Spirit as noticeable aspects of our lives. We will erect barriers to the experience of God. In the deep loneliness that creates, we will do almost anything to feel alive, worthwhile, indispensable, or numb. Life is hard and barren when we push back against the good. This is especially true when we decide we have no choice or that the good is really not good after all. Then we can find ourselves "deteriorating faster than we can lower our own standards, as Anne Lamott recounts a friend saying at his rock-bottom moment in his battle with alcoholism.[15] That perfectly describes our situations when we resist the Spirit in favor of lesser gods.

SELF-LOVE AND SELF-CONTROL

The paradox at the heart of self-control is that our capacity for self-control depends on our ability to truly love ourselves with all our imperfections. Sinful behavior often arises from deep-seated or unrecognized fear, loneliness, or self-hatred. They become fixations that keep us from seeing what is really true about ourselves and others. They are self-abandonment that render us unable to see what the Spirit is doing at our core because we no longer know who we are at our core. Even Calvin, who considered depravity to be at the heart of human experience, did not consider it as defining us. The image of God is present and discernible in each person, even in our floundering state. Sin is never who we really are. It is an ill-fitting suit.

Sin is often linked to the stories we tell ourselves when we are hurting and how we wrongly try to rewrite them. Few of us choose sinful behavior for its own sake. Layers of pain, confusion, or downright resistance to our own unique selves and the moral boundaries of God's values always underlie our choices. We choose to act sinfully when we are trying to be autonomous or not to hurt, not to feel, or not to be limited; when we feel shame that we can't transmute; or maybe, too, when we are dealing with overwhelming disappointment or helplessness. Whatever the spark, when we find ourselves living outside our deepest values and God's deepest values, it is untenable. Self-control can help us claw our way back to coherence and peace.

To exercise the fruit of mature self-control is an act of self-love and self-respect. It requires the capacity to remain in discomfort for a larger purpose. Obviously that purpose is to mature in Christ and to be usable disciples. It is also to heal the soul. Spirit-powered self-control helps perfect us. In his teaching about loving enemies,

Jesus tells us to "be perfect, therefore, as your heavenly Father is perfect" (Matt. 5:48). "Perfect" does not mean without fault or blemish. It means whole, complete, fully grown, or mature.

Sometimes the enemy of our wholeness is within. It may come in the guise of unrealistic expectations of ourselves, toxic or exaggerated thought processes, fears, or poor self-worth. We can't forgive ourselves for not living our lives perfectly, nor for not achieving what we want for ourselves or our families, so we harden our hearts toward ourselves. We change our names to Failure, Bitter, Unlovable, Disappointment. The role of evil is to lie, and those things are all lies. Still, fear and negativity can stick to our nerve endings and distort how we view ourselves and whether we think we are even worth controlling.

Once I had a vivid dream that I pondered repeatedly for many years. I dreamed that I was in a dungeon, seated with many other people at a long medieval table. There were weapons all along the walls. It was dark and damp. I looked nothing like myself. I was a short, squatty little creature with armor, a Viking hat with horns, and scissor hands. The table was spread with food, but with my scissor hands, I could not eat. Others around the table either mocked or ignored me. Jesus was at the head of the table, and he didn't seem to notice the problem. Rather, he went around the table and showed each of the other guests how to use a special spoon. Little Scissor Hands was in despair. She was too defective to even be a part of the banquet. At Jesus' signal, one by one, each of the other guests offered Little Scissor Hands a choice delicacy from the table. As she ate, her demeanor changed. She became radiant and sat up straight. The light in the dungeon began to change, and her armor disappeared. What had begun as a hidden place of suffering, isolation, and incapacity became an inner council of grace.

As I pondered that dream, I began to think of each person around the table as an aspect of myself from which I was cut off due to fear or self-loathing. Each part of us has a gift to offer the whole of us. This is true even of the parts that frighten us or that we have locked away to deal with later when we have time and luxury. The things we reject about ourselves have a blessing to offer if we are brave enough to attend the inner banquet.

Many of those parts that frighten or shame us just want a hug in order to take their rightful, helpful place in our soul. Allowing the wonders of who we are to dine with the less-than-stellar parts gives us room to deal with our failures and faults. It allows us to discover what the need is that our sinful choices inappropriately try to meet, and to experience the powerful grace of forgiveness which softens the soil of the soul so that the Spirit's garden can grow. If self-love is the potting soil for self-control, forgiveness is the fertilizer.

Self-control is helped by developing the grace of self-acceptance of both our weaknesses and our strengths. It rests on self-appreciation and self-surrender in equal measures. Spirit self-control gives us the gift of being able to manage our emotions and reactions. It helps us to walk mindfully through our tangle of feelings, to embrace them and learn from them, without being in bondage to them. It gives us the freedom to decide not to do everything we feel like doing the instant we feel like doing it. It also allows us to choose to do what is needful, even if we don't feel like it.

When we do the sacred inner work of wholeness, we find that self-control is also self-care. At some point in our lives, many of us experience a howling inner ache. If we allow ourselves to notice it at all, we might call it loneliness or disappointment or shame. We will do a lot of different hurtful things to address that ache, quell it, or exorcise it. That ache will be the place where our sin arises nine times out of ten, and the place most needing self-control. It is also where self-control is most grace-filled. When we understand our capacity to manage our longings, fears, and pains, the world opens up as a fresh and gracious space. Spirit then inspires our actions and inactions for the best for everyone. That is mercy of the highest order. Mercy is automatic, but opening to it, especially through the fruit of self-control, is not.

What is it in the human heart that tends to reject mercy we feel we do not deserve? Whatever it is longs to be examined and released, or it will rule us and strangle out the fruit of the Spirit. As we face the truth of who we are created to be and deal with those things that obstruct who the Spirit is making us, paradoxically we cease being self-centered and therefore become freer to love ourselves and others. Self-control is the capacity to choose to do no harm, either to ourselves or to our neighbor.

SELF-CONTROL
AND LOVE OF NEIGHBOR

Spirit self-control rises from an indomitable respect for God's creation in all its diversity. It includes our own lives and processes and extends to the entire human family and to the earth itself. When we show self-control by consciously choosing not to engage in behaviors that are harmful to us, we naturally realize that behaviors that are harmful to others or the planet can no longer be a part of our lives. When we mature in the fruit of the Spirit, we find that we cannot love ourselves and simultaneously harm, dismiss, or oppress others. We cannot live in freedom when others are being held captive. We cannot exploit the natural resources of the planet or refuse to acknowledge truths we wish weren't true. We cannot master our own passions and dispel our own delusions while at the same time exercising no restraint for the good of others. That kind of self-centered binary will kill us all. Buddhists call this living in the illusion of separateness. In Jesus' high priestly prayer on the night of his betrayal, he passionately asks God to make the people one as he and the Father are one (John 17:21). There really is no us and them. What we do to one, we do to all, including ourselves.

Sometimes self-control is needed in order for us to remember that we are one during agitated times of division and vitriol. Self-control teaches us to control our thoughts, our judgments, and our fear. It trains our hearts to see the good in others and lift it up. We master our tongues and our passions so that they do not leave their bounds and consume us or others. With the Spirit's power, we master our tendency to kill with a word, a look, a rumor, or a weapon. When we activate Spirit self-control, we say and do only that which is needed and loving for others and ourselves.

In a clamoring world with overwhelming need, self-control allows us to tame the tyranny of the urgent, but only if our egos are not in charge. Our egos love the urgent. It makes us feel powerful and indispensable when we leap into every void. At least it does until we crash and burn. Self-control allows us to take a breath and listen for the Spirit's promptings and not the adrenaline rush of having to do everything right this moment. That rush itself can be as addictive as any other chemical. Self-control teaches us that we are not the only ones God has to work with. Nor are we just a random bundle of nerve endings put at complete service to our schedules and immediate desires while the needs of others get lost in the flurry.

Self-control is the Spirit's power that makes it possible to remain in the hard places for the common good when running would seem warranted. It also allows us to exit when we can only do additional harm. It is hard to find and live from our true Spirit-indwelt selves when habits, pathways, and institutions on which we have relied to navigate the world crumble. It is hard to remain in difficulty for a higher good when we are disappointed and feel betrayed. Jesus must have wrestled with this himself in the Garden of Gethsemane when Judas betrayed him with a kiss and again when Peter betrayed him in the courtyard of his inquisition. And yet he controlled his hurt and found his "nevertheless" moment. In the presence of anything that is happening within us and around us, the Spirit gives us the capacity to, with Jesus, say "nevertheless" and move forward with actions that are loving, brave, and balanced. Self-control itself is a risk. It is also a sure pathway to freedom.

CONCLUSION

When I was a young pastor in Colorado, our family got an Old English sheepdog puppy named Jubilee. She was beautiful and loving. She also had to be tamed. So she and I went diligently to puppy obedience training, where we were both trained to restrain impulses that would only harm our relationship. Jubilee excelled.

One Sunday, after Jubilee graduated, I decided that I wanted to use her as an object lesson for a children's sermon. I was working with the Scripture passage about Jesus as a shepherd who knows our names (John 10). I arranged for one of my elders to hold Jubilee in sit-stay position in the narthex until I called her name. I could see her, but the children could not. She was bursting with energy. At just the right moment, I called her and gave the hand signal for her to come to me. She ran down the aisle hindfoot over fore and leapt in my lap, tipping me over backward, and licked my face. I think of that as a picture of the boundless joy of learning self-control. Jubilee did not want to wait in the narthex. She did not want to sit quietly in the presence of a lot of stimulation. But she had learned that the reward for doing that far surpassed the challenge of holding back. She was a picture of joyful self-control in fur.

Paul brackets his list of fruit of the Spirit in Galatians 5 with love at the beginning and self-control at the end. Each characteristic is like a window into which we look and see an aspect of God. Some scholars argue that that is not the case with self-control. They say that because God cannot be tempted to do a wrong thing, self-control is not needed and therefore not a part of who God is. I can see that point. I also see Jesus, God in skin, exercising tremendous self-control throughout his ministry. He constantly waited for the right time, stayed in conversations with those who wished him ill, submitted to Pilate with calm control, and found just the right times to express his emotions. Whether we think of God needing to somehow restrain God's own impulses, clearly Jesus models the strength and freedom of self-control. His self-control led to the joyous freedom of the empty tomb.

A WEEK FOR TENDING
SELF-CONTROL

Day One: "Some days later when Felix came with his wife Drusilla, who was Jewish, he sent for Paul and heard him speak concerning faith in Christ Jesus. And as he discussed justice, self-control, and the coming judgment, Felix became frightened and said, 'Go away for the present'" (Acts 24:24–25). Sometimes the prospect of real self-control can be daunting. I remember years ago when I went to a Weight Watchers meeting. All I wanted to do was sit in the back and cry. I have heard people with all kinds of addictions say similar things. They want to quit, but the thought of living without the substance is terrifying. Ponder today whether there are any habits in your life that need to change. What are your feelings about changing them? Tell God exactly how you feel and ask the Holy Spirit to unleash an amazing spirit of self-control in you. The Spirit will give you just enough for today, and that is enough. Take a moment at bedtime to review the choices you made today. In what ways did you make faithful choices? What choices were less than perfect? Did you feel any new bursts of self-control? If so, thank God. If not, ask for more help tomorrow.

Day Two: "For this very reason, you must make every effort to support your faith with excellence, and excellence with knowledge, and knowledge with self-control, and self-control with endurance, and endurance with godliness, and godliness with mutual affection, and mutual affection with love" (2 Pet. 1:5–7). Self-control is a crucial link in the chain of the spiritual life that moves our often-timid belief into the realm of deep love of God, others, and even ourselves. Without that link, we can get stuck along the way and lose the felt experiences of love and wisdom that God has given to us in Christ Jesus. In what ways do you find self-control difficult in the spiritual life? Are some spiritual practices easier for you to make into habits than others? If so, celebrate the Spirit's self-control already at work in you! If worship attendance has become a habit, that is the Spirit exercising self-control in you. If you pray each morning and evening, that is self-control. The Spirit gives the power, but we must make the choice to put self-control to work. At bedtime tonight, thank God for the moments today when you exercised self-control. Ask for this fruit to grow in you tomorrow.

Day Three: "For a bishop [overseer], as God's steward, must be blameless; he must not be arrogant or quick-tempered or addicted to wine or violent or greedy for gain, but he must be hospitable, a lover of goodness, self-controlled, upright, devout, and restrained" (Titus 1:7–8). Self-control is an essential quality of leadership. Whether we are called into leadership positions in the church or not, all of us as believers lead by example in our daily lives. How might growth in self-control make your life more productive, powerful, or influential? How do you think that people see you? How do other people feel when they are with you? If they feel more holy, safe, and inspired, then you are probably living with a good deal of self-control. If they feel nervous, uncertain, or confused, it may be that you lack self-control and so they never know what to expect from you. Before bed, think for a moment of the ways that you have led by example today. Were there times you held your tongue? Times you took good care of yourself or others? Thank God for those times. Ask, also, that tomorrow you will be able to live with more awareness and self-control than today.

Day Four: "I will be your father, and you shall be my sons and daughters, says the Lord Almighty" (2 Cor. 6:18). The word we translate as "Almighty" comes from the same root as our word for self-control. It means strength that holds all things together. In this section of Paul's letter, he is cautioning the people in Corinth to be very careful about their interactions with unbelievers. He knows, as we do, that behavior is often contagious. It is easier for us to do something, whether or not it is moral or in our best spiritual interest, when others are doing the same thing. Are there people or circumstances in your life that make self-control harder for you? Are there people who make it hard for you to resist gossip when you are with them? Are there people who seem to draw you into their "drama"? Are there people or events that make it harder for you to eat right or drink responsibly? Make a list of these people or situations. Don't worry about trying to "fix" it right now. Just ask God for greater awareness. With that awareness will come a fresh resolve, and before you know, it you will be limiting those situations or taking control of your behavior in them.

Day Five: "Jesus began to weep" (John 11:35). Exercising self-control does not negate our emotions. It is impossible—and dangerous to our mental, emotional, physical, and spiritual health to try—to overly suppress our emotions. We have them for a reason, and so did Jesus. He was not a stoic kind of guy. He felt grief, anger, joy, frustration, triumph, and abandonment. So do we. Self-control does not come by trying to force ourselves to remain impassive. Self-control comes by choosing to stick to our values and live with integrity in the midst of any emotional situation. Do you ever berate yourself for your emotional responses to circumstances or people? Do you ever feel that you are too emotional or that you lack empathy? How might the Spirit fruit of self-control help you in your emotional health? At bedtime, thank God that you are created in God's own image with the full range of emotions and aspirations. Ask God to show you exactly what disciplines of the faith (prayer, study, service, etc.) you should develop more fully. Choose one and make a commitment as to how you will approach it in the morning.

Day Six: "Athletes exercise self-control in all things; they do it to receive a perishable wreath, but we an imperishable one" (1 Cor. 9:25). To receive the full bounty of the Christian life requires self-control and discipline. Just as athletes discipline themselves in order to be their best and to have a competitive edge, as Christians we discipline ourselves for rewards both here and in heaven. In fact, when we choose to faithfully worship, study, serve, pray, and reflect, God brings us a little bit of heaven on earth. Our joy overflows. Our blessings increase. Our capacity to love deepens. Our compassion and energy for service explodes. Are there elements of your Christian "training program" that have grown lax? Where do you need to recommit and reconnect? Without thinking too hard, make a list of the first things that come into your mind when you pray, "Lord, show me what I need most." Pray through that list whenever it comes to mind today. Offer it to God and ask for guidance and the perfect opportunities for you.

Questions for Reflection and Discussion

1. When you think about the power of self-control in your life, in what circumstances do you exercise it most? Where would you want the Spirit to mature self-control in you?

2. Self-control is personal. It comes to maturity in each of us. It is also a Spirit characteristic of the church, of groups, and even of cultures. How do you see self-control as operative in those groups? Where do you see it lacking? What are some of the tangible results?

3. Paul seems to see self-control as the medicine needed to combat sin. How do you see that operate?
4. A part of the character of self-control is bravery. Can you think of a time when you controlled your fear of hurt in order to do something brave?
5. Self-control is often exercised in vulnerability. What helps you remain in necessary situations even if you feel vulnerable?
6. Was there anything in the chapter that surprised you? If so, how?

CONCLUSION

Joy is the Echo of God's life in us.
—Columba of Iona

In a wild flurry of inspiration born out of frustration and love, Paul paints a picture for the Galatian church, and us, of a way of life for which we were born and redeemed. To make it more starkly compelling, he begins by telling us what is not included, what will suffocate us, what will decimate our inner gardens. When we go to the deep places in Scripture, we can sometimes feel that our lives fall so far short of the standard that we wish we never knew what we have learned. Just stay the course. Even if your garden seems fallow, the Spirit is working in the dark, doing what is needed for growth.

Few of us experience the fruit all the time or all at once. An orchard must be planted. Vines must be tended. Sunlight and water must be provided, and weeds and pests must be dealt with, for roots to establish and become durable. It is helpful to remember that the Spirit does not demand great actions of will in order to manifest the fruit. All that is needed is surrender, openness, gratitude, and a willingness to look at our truth and release the toxins we find into God's healing grace.

In doing work with the Spirit's fruit, we can find ourselves in the strange and foreign experience of living in two worlds at once. The vices and the virtues, in some sense, cohabitate in our awareness while the garden is maturing, even as we know they are ultimately incompatible. Paul puts it this way: "I do not understand my own actions. For I do not do what I want, but I do the very thing I hate" (Rom. 7:15). Maybe that is why in the parable of the Weeds among the Wheat, Jesus tells his friends to let the weeds grow with the wheat so that we don't damage the good by trying to eradicate the bad.

Even when we approach the Spirit with our lives in tatters, the miracle of the Spirit's garden is that we can always start again. Maybe when Jesus refers to blasphemy against the Holy Spirit, he is just referring to thinking that you can't start over, that you are too old, too sinful, too willful, too weak, to change. This is resoundingly untrue! One of the clearest and most winsome demonstrations of the power and presence of the Spirit is a transformed life, and it is available to all of us. The fruit of the Spirit is not a destination. It is a signpost on the way to our true destination, which is union with God, oneness, salvation, wholeness. The fruit is what the Spirit does in us, with our agreement, to show us where we are headed.

At some point, our egos dissolve into the fruit and we sink down into our true selves, tucked into the heart of Christ. That true self is always in a state of fruitfulness and becomes part of the flow of Spirit work in the world. We become both more and less than we think we are. We find that we are tangibly indwelt. It is not often a goose-pimply mountaintop experience kind of thing. At least it is not for me. It is more like sugar dissolving into sweet tea. It is still tea, still dripping with condensation, just sweeter, less caustic, hinting at unknown beauties happening unseen all around. Once we recognize the Spirit's fruit and glimpse it in our lives, we will become uncomfortable when we do not experience it flowing.

The fruit of the Spirit is not for our lives alone. It is not just for the prayer closet or personal healing from trauma and confusion. It is a way that the Spirit continues to work in the world through us, one delicious inner experience at a time. It is important to share the fruit with others, because as any gardener knows, any healthy garden produces far more fruit than any one person can possibly eat. The Spirit's garden as it matures draws us inward and propels us outward with equal magnetic pull. When prayer and action are fused, fruit flourishes and we begin to live into something, individually and together, that our hearts and minds can never contain. We can only tend and release.

The nuances and shape the fruit takes in us will be varied, unique, and perfect for us and for our life's mission. Perhaps we will awaken to the fruit in the order in which Paul offers his words. After all, is joy possible without love? Is peace possible without love and joy? But perhaps it will be totally different, like pick-up sticks, and will include additional aspects of Spirit fruit that Paul doesn't mention. It will become evident over time. Just as the lines on my face are evidence of seventy years of choices made, the choices we make daily to tend the Spirit's garden are cumulative and will be evident in our lives.

Whatever our stumbling blocks in life may be, the Spirit's fruit will address them. Why? Because each aspect of the fruit of the Spirit is a window through which we can gaze at God more intimately and see how God is working with and within us. Everything fits. Nothing is broken; nothing is missing.

When we recognize the depth and power of the Spirit's fruit in our lives, something emerges, like a sturdy bud bursting through hard ground. Even the air we breathe, like the *ruach* Spirit-breath that hovered over the waters of creation, seems to burst open, and something sacred passes between us and the Spirit, between us and others, and between us and ourselves. That is indeed a healing journey that requires clearing the ground of the delusions and sin that can run rampant beneath the surface. It is well worth the continued effort.

A friend once told me that when a caterpillar forms a chrysalis and begins the process of transformation, it does not just sprout wings on its old body. Rather, it dissolves completely into a kind of goo she called butterfly soup. From that dissolved state, the new creature emerges in its time. For the fruit of the Spirit to transform and heal us, sometimes it takes waiting in butterfly soup until wings form and stretch. It takes pushing through the dark and facing all the wild elements of truth. It takes pruning our old views, worn masks, and frayed certainties. It takes new growth that is the only thing strong enough to bear the world's sorrow, and our own, with a hope that laughs even at the grave. It takes supernatural intimacy with the One who made us, knows us, loves us, and whose only perfect desire is our wholeness.

This book cannot do that for you. Nor can even your most concerted efforts. My prayer, even so, is that this writing may prickle you aware of your own interior garden and that you will put on your garden gloves and dig deeply. You will be met by the Spirit every step of the way. That is a promise. How could it be otherwise?

It is, after all, all about grace. Just grace.

NOTES

1. Richard Rohr, *What the Mystics Know* (New York: Crossroad, 2015), 29.

2. Belden C. Lane has an interesting discussion of the ramifications of this in his book *Ravished by Beauty: The Surprising Legacy of Reformed Spirituality* (Oxford: Oxford University Press, 2011). See especially, chap. 1.

3. Sebastian Gendry, "120 Inspirational Quotes about Laughter," Laughter Online University (website), accessed October 26, 2023, https://www.laughteronlineuniversity.com/quotes-about-laughter/.

4. "Elizabeth Barrett Browning Quotes," BrainyQuote.com, Brainy Media Inc., 2024, https://www.brainyquote.com/quotes/elizabeth_barrett_brownin_387342, accessed April 22, 2024.

5. "Michelango Quotes," BrainyQuote.com, Brainy Media Inc., 2004, https://www.brainyquote.com/quotes/michelangelo_161309, accessed October 26, 2023.

6. *The Book of Common Worship* (Louisville, KY: Westminster John Knox Press, 2018), 1109.

7. Patrick Hart, ed., *The Other Side of the Mountain: The End of the Journey* (New York: HarperCollins, 1998), 323.

8. Frances Hodgson Burnett, *Little Lord Fauntleroy* (New York: Charles Scribner's Sons, 1907), 138.

9. "John Lewis Quotes," BrainyQuotes.com, BrainyMedia Inc., 2024, https://www.brainyquote.com/quotes/john_lewis_810315, accessed April 16, 2024.

10. James Baldwin, "As Much Truth as One Can Bear," *New York Times Book Review,* January 14, 1962.

11. *Book of Common Worship,* 87.

12. "Thomas Aquinas Quotes," BrainyQuotes.com, BrainyMedia Inc., 2024, https://www.brainyquote.com/quotes/thomas_aquinas_186900, accessed April 16, 2024.

13. The source of the story is unknown. It appears in many places, including under "Involvement" in the "Illustration Topics" section of the Family Times website, https://www.family-times.net/illustration/Involvement/201387/, accessed November 2, 2023.

14. "Rabindranath Tagore Quotes," BrainyQuote.com, BrainyMedia Inc., 2004, https://www.brainyquote.com/quotes/rabindranath_tagore_121379, accessed November 2, 2023.

15. Anne Lamott, *Almost Everything* (New York: Riverhead Books, 2018), 70.